se for THINKING LIKE A DIRECTOR

"If I ever decided (heaven and hell forbid) to direct a play, I'd be sure to have Michael Bloom's illuminating and indispensable text nearby to guide and challenge me, step-by-step, as I found my way."
— Ariel Dorfman

"With a relaxed, informal style, *Thinking Like a Director* captures the experience of stage directing as well as any book I can think of. Its section on working with living playwrights is a welcome addition to the literature, useful to playwrights as much as directors, and Bloom's writing on language will be highly informative for actors, too. I would think every drama school would want several copies."
— Arthur Kopit

"It's rare for a 'how-to' book to be at the same time so practical and so literate."
— Robert Brustein, Artistic Director, American Repertory Theatre

"More engaging than a textbook, *Thinking Like a Director* is a concise and highly practical guide to the craft. It's required reading for young stage and film directors, students, and anyone who wants to know what a skillful professional director does."
— Gilbert Cates, Producing Director of the Geffen Playhouse and Producer of the Academy Awards Show

"*Thinking Like a Director* is a lucid, concise, and admirably undogmatic manual for aspirant directors, from which writers, actors, and ordinary theatergoers will also learn much about the complex business of putting on plays."
— ... elist and playwright, of *Changing Places*

In addition to directing throughout the United States and Japan, Michael Bloom is head of directing at the University of Texas at Austin. His writing on the stage has appeared in *The New York Times* and *American Theatre* magazine. Bloom directed the premiere of Donald Margulies's Pulitzer Prize–winning play *Dinner with Friends* at the Actors Theatre of Louisville, and he has also directed premieres by Don DeLillo, Ariel Dorfman, David Hare, and David Lodge. He won the Elliott Norton Award for Directing for his production of *Gross Indecency*, and was nominated for a Drama Desk for *Sight Unseen* at Manhattan Theatre Club and the Orpheum Theatre. He lives in Austin, Texas.

THINKING LIKE A
DIRECTOR

A PRACTICAL HANDBOOK

Michael Bloom

FARRAR, STRAUS AND GIROUX
NEW YORK

Farrar, Straus and Giroux
18 West 18th Street, New York 10011

Grateful acknowledgment is made for permission to reprint excerpts from the
following: "Nora" by Henrik Ibsen from *Ingmar Bergman: A Project for the
Theatre,* copyright © 1983 by Frederick Ungar Publishing Company. Reprinted
by permission of The Continuum International Publishing Group; "The Glass
Menagerie" by Tennessee Williams, copyright 1945 by Tennessee Williams and
Edwina D. Williams. Copyright renewed 1973 by Tennessee Williams. Used by
permission of Random House, Inc.

Library of Congress Cataloging-in-Publication Data
Bloom, Michael, 1950–
    Thinking like a director, a practical handbook / Michael Bloom.—1st ed.
        p.   cm.
    Includes bibliographical references and an index.
    ISBN 978-0-571-19992-1 (alk. paper) — ISBN 978-0-571-19994-5
(pbk. : alk. paper)
        1. Theater — Production and direction—Handbooks, manuals, etc.
    I. Title.

PN2053. B58 2001
792'.0233—dc21

                                                                2001023157

Hardcover ISBN: 978-0-571-19992-1
Paperback ISBN: 978-0-571-19994-5

Designed by Thomas Frank

Our books may be purchased in bulk for promotional, educational, or business
use. Please contact your local bookseller or the Macmillan Corporate and
Premium Sales Department at 1-800-221-7945, extension 5442, or by e-mail at
MacmillanSpecialMarkets@macmillan.com.

www.fsgbooks.com

28   27   26   25   24   23   22   21   20   19   18

For Anne and David

CONTENTS

Preface   ix
Acknowledgments   xi
Introduction   3

I. PREPARATION   9
1. Thinking Like an Artist   11
2. Reading and Researching   17
3. Interpreting the Action   31
4. External Analysis: Structure   46

II. PRE-PRODUCTION   67
5. Developing the Approach   69
6. The Design Process   81
7. Style   95
8. Casting   104

III. REHEARSAL   117
9. The Early Rehearsals   119
10. Staging   140
11. The Middle Rehearsals: Problem Solving   151
12. The External Perspective in Rehearsals   173
13. The Final Stages   184

IV. RESOURCES   197

14. The Directorial Landscape   199

Appendix 1 The Next Project   205
Appendix 2 Sample Rehearsal Timeline   210
Appendix 3 Points of Reference: Scenes from
    The Glass Menagerie and *Nora*   213
Notes   223
Glossary   227
Recommended Reading   231
Index   233

PREFACE

As a fledgling director in New York City, I once took a class from a well-known professional and teacher. He required his students to present scenes, to which he responded after each showing. His comments were always stimulating, and I rarely found myself in disagreement. Yet I was always puzzled. I could never determine how he had arrived at his observations nor how to make future use of them. To me they seemed too idiosyncratic to encourage a particular way of thinking. As I look back, I recognize that class as the beginning of my journey to develop a coherent way of working, and this book is another step in that process.

In using the phrase *thinking like a director*, I don't mean to imply that directing is merely an intellectual process. Rather, successful directors have a theatrical mindset that includes thoughts, feelings, impulses, and sensory responses. What this book offers is a way of thinking about directing that I hope will further your search for a personal approach; a sequence of signposts, not rules; a handbook rather than an instruction manual. It differs from directing textbooks, which rarely reveal the connections between a director's many roles—the way they work in practice. By demonstrating how directors make choices and form instincts, I hope to convey the *experience* of directing.

An important premise of this book is that the mindset of most successful directors incorporates a dual perspective, a concentration both on a play's *internal* facets—the inner life of each character—and on its *external* or structural elements. This bifocal vision clarifies the director's responsibilities to the play and to the audience, with one perspective acting as a check or balance on the other. And it helps integrate the director's tasks, encouraging an organic way of thinking about directing.

Barely a century old, stage directing has quickly transformed itself into a very complex art. As late as the 1950s, books on directing consisted mostly of technical instructions for staging. But as the twentieth century promoted the interpretative function as essential to nearly all human endeavors, directors developed a greater sophistication in analyzing texts and working with actors. These two subjects form the core of this book, because I believe the best directors possess a thorough understanding of how an actor creates a performance.

Thinking Like a Director is intended for students and stage directors at all levels of experience. Film directors can benefit especially from the sections on analysis, action breakdown, interpretation, and working with actors and designers. To track the chapters on action, you may wish to refer to the selected scenes in Appendix 3 from the Tennessee Williams classic *The Glass Menagerie*, which serves as the primary case study. Although the play is relatively realistic in style, the principles set forth in this book apply to any style or genre. I also regularly refer to scene 1 of Ingmar Bergman's *Nora*, a modern adaptation of Ibsen's *A Doll's House*, which is also included in Appendix 3.

ACKNOWLEDGMENTS

Among those I wish to thank are the many students who inspired me to reflect on my own practice and to write this book. For imparting the rigor and perseverance that directing demands—and the power of theater—I am grateful to Nathan Garner and John Chioles. No smaller is my debt to another group—the extraordinary actors with whom I've been so fortunate to work. And to my wife, Carol, for her support of my writing, I owe my deepest thanks and gratitude.

THINKING LIKE A
DIRECTOR

INTRODUCTION

If professions move in cycles of desirability and glamour, then directing is surely in an ascendant phase. In theater and film, training programs have burgeoned, while writers and actors by the dozens parlay
their success into directing. In contrast to the world of conglomerates
and multinationals, directing is a means of creative expression, allowing a single artist a significant measure of control. Its allure is con-
firmed by the ubiquitous memo pad sold in bookshops that bears the
epigram ". . . but what I really want to do is direct."

Yet the nature of a director's work, most notably in the theater,
remains surprisingly vague and mysterious. Audiences generally assume directors tell actors where and when to move and, perhaps,
how to recite certain lines. Critics often think directors are occupied
primarily with speed and pace. Even some actors find it difficult to
characterize the differences between one director's process and another's.

The truth is that there is no one accepted method for directing,
any more than there is for any other art. How a director fares is
greatly dependent on who that person is, his collaborators, and the
project at hand. To complicate matters, the relationship between

product and process isn't always direct and causal. Some directors work themselves to the bone, while others do very little. Paradoxically, there is success and failure in both categories. But it would be naïve not to believe that *most* successful productions occur because of the intensive efforts of a skilled director. As this book's title indicates, a crucial step in acquiring and utilizing those skills is developing a particular way of thinking.

PREREQUISITES

An actor friend once asked my advice on whether he should become a director. He'd spent some years playing mostly less-than-rewarding roles and now wanted greater artistic control. He was a smart, talented performer who was attuned to the subtleties of the rehearsal process. His experience in acting and coaching others in scenes and auditions suggested that his knowledge of behavior and his intuitive sense of the dramatic would give him a head start. But that was all I knew about his qualifications.

When I said I wasn't sure how to advise him, he seemed puzzled. I explained that the actor-director interaction in rehearsals is often very different from coaching. As evidence, I cited how rarely master acting teachers become accomplished directors. Did he have an appreciation for narrative, I asked, an instinct for staging, a strong visual imagination, an innate musicality, a critical facility, a background in theater history, and an ability to take the heat, ride the lows, and keep a level head around praise and criticism? While he certainly possessed some of these attributes, he confessed to not realizing the extent of the directorial job description.

The seminal American director Elia Kazan once put forward a far more daunting list of prerequisites that included expertise in economics, warfare, religion, food, travel, sports, and a host of other subjects. His point was that to create the world of a play, to sew a whole cloth from the threads of language, a director has to know a good deal about many things. For the director and critic Harold Clurman, the job entailed being "an organizer, a teacher, a politician, a psychic detective, a lay analyst, a technician, a creative being . . . All of which means he must be a great lover." A director is a medium—between actors and text, between the text and the physical elements, and of course between the producer and the production.

Directing demands polymaths, those who are at home in a library, a rehearsal hall, a production meeting, and a producer's office. To construct entire worlds and coordinate so many elements, you must have an appreciation for literature, an understanding of the actor's craft, and a visual and verbal acuity. Other than an orchestra conductor, no other artist is as dependent on the contributions of others. Ultimately, the director is a creator of communities—someone who can recognize talent and inspire the very best from other artists, lead them but welcome their contributions, and make everyone feel they are important partners.

THE DIRECTOR AS STORYTELLER

In the most basic terms, the director is a production's primary storyteller. A play has only one plot (including subplots), but it contains many potential stories. The interpretation of the primary characters largely determines the story, so in effect, every production of the same play will inevitably tell a different tale. One of the most important functions a director fulfills is determining, with the actors and designers, which story to tell and how to tell it coherently.

As plots have become less linear, the job of telling a story has grown more complicated. While postmodernism and other aesthetics have increased our awareness of the disjunctions inherent in most stories, they have also incited some to reject identification between characters and audience—and even storytelling itself—as passé. At the same time, many artists, in theater, film, and novels, have demonstrated that coherent stories can accommodate contradictions and reflect a fragmented world.

One instinct in particular is indispensable to storytelling: the ability to discover what delights an audience. Throughout his writings, Peter Brook, one of the extraordinary minds of the modern theater, recounts how each time his ensemble of actors visited a remote corner of the world, whether a village, a hospital, or an open field, they were obliged to relearn how to hold an audience's attention. No matter how ambitious or experimental his work, Brook has never drifted far from the simple question of what makes an audience respond. If this ability seems basic to doing theater, it is all too often absent in practice. Some time ago I attended a performance by a local ensemble that advertised stylized, cutting-edge theater based on new acting theories but actually produced a cartoon that completely concealed the performers as human beings. The play was meant to be a comedy, yet when I scanned the room, only the stage managers, seated behind me, were laughing. The production was raucous but completely failed to entertain because the actors and director were far too absorbed in celebrating their process to gauge the audience's attention.

THE DIRECTOR AS ANIMATOR

Nearly everything a director does is in the service of animating the story. To that end, most successful directors employ twin points of view simultaneously. One consists of living inside the play, discovering its energy by probing and empathizing with the characters' deepest desires and flaws; the other is a focus on structure.

By analogy, if we were to examine an automobile closely, we'd want to look at it from both inside and outside. We would study its engine to learn how it runs, and scrutinize its design to determine its structure. This dual perspective would disclose far more than describing its color or accessories, which, in analyzing a play, would correspond to merely hunting for themes rather than probing more deeply for the inner workings of a play—its motor.

Like many actors, most directors work from the inside out *and* the outside in. On the one hand, using action, obstacle, and given circumstances, most skillful directors animate the acting with a vocabulary that is organic to most actors. But they also concentrate on the play's structural or external elements, including its central conflict, function, event, architecture, and suspense. As this book strives to demonstrate, in a dynamic directorial mindset these two angles of vision work in tandem, with each balancing the other.

PART I

PREPARATION

ONE

THINKING LIKE AN ARTIST

S ome textbooks and directing courses give the impression that a director's proficiency in certain skills, such as staging and composition, translates into great productions. But as with every art, technique alone is hardly sufficient. To be successful, a director must be creative, inventive, intuitive, and above all passionate. Passion is what energizes the director's search for the animus or inner life of a play. Without an enthusiasm for sharing stories, relating deeply to characters becomes laborious if not impossible, and directors who lack this passion tend to produce bloodless work. Just as an actor should have an ax to grind (a strong intention) when she comes onstage, the director-artist must have something to say. It need not be a social or political statement, and it should not replace or subordinate what *the play* has to say. It simply means a passion for communicating with a unique point of view. Having something to say is having a reason to tell a story, a reason to direct.

Not long ago American directing was regarded more as a craft than as an art. In this environment, a background in literature and ideas was considered detrimental (in contrast to the English theater, where many directors used to prepare by reading philosophy at Oxford or Cambridge). A recent American comedy amusingly satirized the director as someone obsessed with making minute changes in the placement of furniture. But as the directorial profile has evolved from manager or craftsperson to full-fledged artist—not unlike the development of film directing—professional theaters genuinely committed to artistry have hired directors for their sensibility, taste, and vision—in other words, for their aesthetic. These attributes are very difficult to teach; paradoxically, they're best acquired by studying subjects other than theater.

Peter Falk once said that "an actor must be in love with ambiguity." And so must a director, if he is to be an artist. "The great feature of the theatre," said Peter Brook, "is that the audience can enter very deeply into contradictions." By entering one point of view deeply and then another, he adds, "you can see what you can really do in life." In contrast to the media-dominated world of hype, speed, and sound-byte attention spans, theater has the potential to offer visions that are messy and conflicting, full and complex.

A former artistic director of the Guthrie Theater, Garland Wright, described the sea change that occurred in his thinking when he first went to work as an associate director under the previous artistic director, Liviu Ciulei. According to Wright, Ciulei was

> the person who made me choose whether to be a *director* or an *artist* . . . "Artist" is a word that floats in your head, but there's a point where you've got to come out of the closet and say, "That's what I intend to be," and saying that rules out a lot of things you might have done in your life. I suppose for me it meant defining the difference between "putting on plays" and participating in the world through theatre. When you make a choice like that, you have to make a commitment to treasure the work—the work above all else, the importance of the work, the seriousness of the work, hopefully the value of the work.

Thinking like a director entails far more than deciding where to place the furniture. It means knowing and accepting the responsibility of an art form. It requires a passion, intelligence, and sensibility as potent as the author's. Not every production can be as powerfully affecting as a Greek tragedy was for a fifth-century Athenian audience, but a director who is also an artist is always reexamining the possibilities of the theatrical form. Only when theater fails to live up to its potential does this sacred sense of purpose seem pretentious. If a director is to think like an artist, she must always be engaged in investigating the power and purpose of theater.

THE DIRECTOR AS INTERPRETER

Although early directing textbooks hardly mentioned interpretation, it is now recognized as central to the director's work, informing every aspect of preparation and production. This progression is a late-twentieth-century phenomenon, occurring, not coincidentally, after the rise of relativism and psychoanalytic theory. In the theater, the reexamination of the classics by directorial titans such as Peter Brook, Ingmar Bergman, Peter Stein, and Giorgio Strehler; the American avant-garde movement of the late 1960s; and the emergence of modern directorial training have all contributed to a growing appreciation of the director's interpretive function.

On the most basic level, interpretation is necessary because language carries multiple meanings. Even a simple question such as "Can you take the bus to the store?" has more than one interpretation. The situation of a play is far more complex, especially as it takes on new sets of meanings after a playwright is no longer in attendance during rehearsals. Using the word "afterlife" in his excellent book *Subsequent Performances*, the British director Jonathan Miller describes this transformation:

> Inevitably with time there comes a point when the human link between the first production and any subsequent one snaps, and the bridge of reminiscence and anecdote is irreparably broken. When that happens the detailed additional instructions that had been written down in the prompt

copy become curiously unintelligible, since there is no one available to explain the generative principles on which they were based. It is at this point that the play begins to enter its afterlife and the indeterminacy of the text begins to assert itself.

Producing a play in its afterlife requires significant interpretation because of the difficulty of divining a deceased author's intention. You don't have to subscribe to fashionable critical theories to recognize that a playwright's written instructions, while sometimes useful, are rarely complete and not always practical. It would take hundreds of pages of notes to convey what is meant by every line of a play, yet what a playwright normally leaves to posterity is a set of declarations meant to deflect criticism, or to support or counter the tendencies of the original production. When followers of a playwright have tried to foster an orthodoxy based on their personal knowledge of the original production, the results have often been stultifying. For example, to see how the plays of Chekhov and Brecht were produced after their deaths—at the Moscow Art Theatre and the Berliner Ensemble, respectively—is to understand that a personal connection to an author does not guarantee a vibrant production. Just as misguided are the claims for presenting Shakespeare "as it was originally produced." These productions tend to be theme park novelties based on scant historical evidence that is in itself open to wide interpretation. Besides, even if we knew exactly how a playwright's work was originally produced, these methods would appear hopelessly quaint when viewed through a contemporary lens.

Some people discount the need to make a play live for a specific audience, yet theater has no choice but to be contemporary. Because audience perception changes with time, interpreting a play necessarily involves making choices about what it means in the present. Theater couldn't remain a living art form if it failed to acknowledge that audiences themselves are engaged in interpretation. Much of the excitement in producing a period play lies in exploring how it lines up with the zeitgeist. After all, theatrical performance is a living, breathing object in the particular world in which it is created. Denying the present curtails a play's resonance, effectively consigning it as a museum artifact. When I approach a play from another era, even a classic, I like to imagine that it has arrived over the transom direct from the author, without the benefit of a celebrated history. In other words, every production should prompt the question *How do I—as a director in my time—make this play work?* At the same time, a play's integrity in production depends on a director's adopting a sensible approach to interpretation that, for Jonathan Miller, and most accomplished directors, takes into account "common sense, tact, and literary sensitivity." Directing *Hamlet* as a comedy would clearly be in violation of these guidelines.

An important goal of my own directing is to discover points of communion between a play and its particular audience in ways that delight and surprise. Changing the original time and place of an older play, a frequent directorial choice, can be effective when it is done with ingenuity and a respect for the audience. But making a play live for a contemporary audience doesn't justify any and all choices, such as automatically transposing it to a contemporary setting, a practice—especially popular in the 1970s—that can destroy a play's complexity.

The director as artist always owes—and must balance—obligations to her aesthetic and to the play. Being creative and humble before a play's essence is one of directing's supreme challenges. There is a thin but recognizable line between this perspective and that of the *auteur* who uses a play to promote an aesthetic, an agenda, or a reputation, presenting, in effect, a gloss on a play rather than the play itself. At the same time, productions such as the Wooster Group's imaginative revisions of *Three Sisters* and *The Crucible* possess a validity that stems in part from the fact that they are clearly presented as new works (with new titles) created by a director.

With a new script, a director's interpretative latitude is generally narrower, especially with the playwright at rehearsals. Having directed the premieres of many new plays, I can attest to the value of having an author share his motivation or intentions behind a work.

Knowing the writer personally can only help the director grasp her point of view and the imaginative world of the play.

But because a playwright isn't usually an actor or designer, his suggestions often need to be reworded, or even interpreted. Occasionally an author may not even know or remember the original basis for a phrase or circumstance. When Peter Hall was directing one of Harold Pinter's early plays, he asked him in rehearsal about a particularly gnarly moment. Pinter paused—of course—and then confessed that the playwright's intention behind the moment had been lost! When the playwright isn't present, the need to interpret her directives is even greater. This is made strikingly clear by seeing how different two (or more) productions of the same play can be, even when guided by a playwright's virtually identical instructions.

The interpretive responsibility can seem daunting even to an experienced director. But it need not be arbitrary if it includes the director's two perspectives: an examination of the characters' actions (the internal view) balanced by a grasp of the play's structure (the external side). The following four chapters attempt to demystify interpretation by breaking it down into a number of components. Ultimately, the best directors come to realize that the interpretive task, though great, is not theirs alone. They recognize their collaborators—actors, designers, and technicians—as partners in the process.

TWO

READING AND RESEARCHING

For a director, no reading of a play is as important as the first, because the experience will most closely mirror that of the average audience. The narrative will unfold in surprising ways, and if the director is drawn to the play, much of its intended impact will be revealed. In rehearsals, when I am puzzled by a scene, I try to recall what it made me feel when I first read it.

Unless I'm uncertain about whether to direct a play, I'm not overly analytical in my first reading, taking Harold Clurman's advice to "let the play work on you before you work on it." I make sure the first reading is pleasurable by finding a comfortable place to sit, without distractions. If possible, I try to get through the play in a single sitting; if I don't, I may not be interested enough to spend several months with it. Directing requires a reservoir of energy and a sense of urgency and commitment. Faced with all the obstacles to giving birth to a play, a writer has determined that this story needs to be told. Without a similar sense of urgency, a director will find it difficult to bring that story to life.

Having read the play and enjoyed it, my mind alive with ideas and images, I then proceed with further readings, research, and analysis. These steps are interdependent and often simultaneous. After reading the play once or twice, I also look up the meanings of words that are unclear or ambiguous. (There is nothing more embarrassing than being asked, at a first rehearsal, the meaning of an unfamiliar word.) With the availability of a wide variety of dictionaries, modern and historical, even the most obscure text can be deciphered.

THE DIRECTOR AS DETECTIVE

One of the next tasks is to determine and track down the extant versions of the play. If it's Shakespeare, the director should read all editions and acquire what is known as a variorum text—an enormously useful line-by-line compendium of textual variations and explanatory notes.

A surprising number of plays, some quite modern, exist in more than one edition. It's the director's responsibility to unearth all versions and, in consultation with the producer, determine which to use. Variations can occur for a number of reasons: a playwright may have written several endings, as Tennessee Williams often did, or a production script may differ from an earlier- or later-published edition. When I directed Williams's *Sweet Bird of Youth*, I found two very different versions. One of them greatly reduces the character of Boss Finley, the play's antagonist and one of its most colorful characters. Although the other version, with Finley's full character, was somewhat longer, I chose it because it offered a much stronger central conflict between him and the protagonist, Chance Wayne.

With *The Glass Menagerie* a director has the choice of several authorized versions. Comparing the opening moments of two of them provides an interesting example of an early but critical directorial choice. Both versions begin with Tom's address to the audience from the porch, introducing himself as narrator and presenting his family's situation. After the monologue, a small but revealing difference occurs. In the New Directions edition, Amanda calls him to dinner, while in the Dramatists Play Service version, she does not acknowledge him until he sits down at the table, and Williams has given her a short speech to cover the time it takes the actor playing Tom to enter. One of the reasons I chose the Dramatists edition when I directed the play was that it gracefully covers the transition from monologue to scene. The New Directions script, in which Amanda summons Tom just after his monologue, contains an awkward pause while Tom moves from the porch to the dining room and calls unneeded attention to the convention of addressing the audience. It might even appear that Amanda knows he is speaking to them and wants him to come join the play that is going on in the dining room! Not surprisingly, the Dramatists edition is a production script that includes changes Williams made in developing the text in rehearsal.

TIP: STAGE DIRECTIONS

One of the oldest saws in the theater is that actors and directors should cross out all stage directions. This practice stems from an era when the acting editions of plays often included the original stage manager's notes prescribing blocking and line readings. But nowadays, when playwrights oversee publication of their works, all editions are more likely to contain only works the writer has invented or approved. To cross out stage directions in Pinter, Beckett, or many other modern writers would be to eliminate a significant facet of their plays. Even a stage direction that prescribes a line reading, while intrusive and perhaps unusable, may offer a clue as to the action the author intended at that moment.

PLAYS IN THE PUBLIC DOMAIN

Generally, plays under copyright cannot be cut, but with a play that is no longer under copyright and thus in the public domain, a director may find it desirable to edit lines or sections for the purpose of focus, clarity, and cogency. There may be good reasons for making adjustments to the script. With the noncopyright plays of Wilde and Shaw, for instance, I often simplify or cut very obscure or outdated references. Leaving them in the text could stop a scene cold while the audience attempted to decipher their meanings. It's far more difficult to employ this strategy with Shakespeare: cutting might clarify meaning, but it would do so at the expense of the poetry. Editing must be done with a strong rationale, or it can disfigure the story and confuse an audience.

TRANSLATIONS AND ADAPTATIONS

When you direct a play that has been translated from a foreign language, no decision is more important than the choice of translation. Whether or not a *dramaturg* or assistant is assigned to research the various translations, it's the director's responsibility to be aware of all possibilities in order to make an informed decision. Simply because a translation exists doesn't mean it will be viable for a contemporary audience. Far too often directors content themselves with whatever is available, ignoring awkward or outdated language. Translations by writers who have had no experience with writing dialogue, such as poets and scholars, can be overly literal or so densely poetic that the language seems stilted and the actions hidden. There are also a great many British translations of plays that, while viable in the British theater, employ too many local idioms for an American production. Often such translations also assign dialects other than standard British—such as Irish or Scottish—to lower-class characters. For non-British audiences, this can be confusing or irrelevant.

Today it would be difficult to imagine directing a Constance Garnett translation of Chekhov or a William Archer translation of Ibsen. Though they were the earliest translators of those two great play-wrights and their work was respected and widely produced, their language now feels stilted and arcane, freezing the plays in an early-twentieth-century frame of reference. Fortunately, more modern translations of these two authors do exist. But for so many important foreign writers, a major reason for the lack of contemporary produc-tions of their work is the absence of new translations.

To see how greatly translations can differ, and just how critical to the ultimate effectiveness of a production the choice of translation can be, let's examine a short excerpt from *Creditors* by August Strind-berg in four different published translations. In this psychosexual drama of power and jealousy in marriage, Tekla, a charmingly inde-pendent woman, returns from a trip to confront her jealous and sus-picious husband Adolf, who has been made even more anxious by a talk with Tekla's ex-husband.

First Translation

Adolf: You're a devil. Did you know that?

Tekla: No, I don't know anything about myself.

Adolf: I see. You never give a thought to your own reactions.

Tekla: On the contrary, I never think about anything but myself—I'm a terrible egoist. You're very philosophical all of a sudden!

Adolf: Put your hand on my forehead.

Tekla: Have you been having another brain-storm? Poor head! Let me see what I can do. *Kisses his forehead.* There, is it better now?

Adolf: Yes, it's better now.

Second Translation

The second translation is very similar except for two important differ-ences. Instead of "philosophical," it uses the word "analytical," a much more precise description of Adolf's behavior, though "critical" would have been even better. In the first translation, "brain-storm" is an unfortunate usage that connotes "idea" rather than "headache," which is what Strindberg meant. The second translation replaces it with the equally imprecise "Has my little boy got bugsy-wugsy in his head?" Although the sentence conveys the baby talk of the couple, it seems incongruous to the tone of the scene.

Third Translation

In the third translation, "You're a devil," a nicely direct statement, is replaced by the oddly scientific and detached "You are a female demon," as if Adolf were labeling a species rather than confronting his wife. It retains the unfortunate use of "philosophical" to describe his behavior. And it translates Adolf's "headache" with the dryly vague "Is something disturbing you again? Would you like me to drive away your worries?"

Fourth Translation

This one also uses the imprecise "philosophical." But the writer does much better with Adolf's "headache": "Is he tied up in knots? Shall I make it better?"

All of these translations are now at least thirty years old, and all contain language that to varying degrees seems outmoded. None of them completely communicates the extraordinarily modern and biting byplay of the original. These examples should demonstrate how meticulous with language a director must be; even a single imprecise word can obscure the sense and action of a scene.

TIP: PRODUCTION TRANSLATIONS

Your optimal strategy, when financially possible, is to commission a new translation by a playwright for your production. (If the play is still under copyright, you must obtain permission from the owner.) You can then work closely with the writer before and during rehearsals to shape the translation to that specific production. "Sometimes it takes work on the rehearsal floor to reveal what is really going on in a scene," states one playwright-translator. "This is often the case with Brecht, where the text frequently represents the tip of a rehearsal iceberg." Sometimes a writer who does not speak the original language of a play will be employed to adapt the translated text. A native speaker provides a "literal" translation, which the writer then adapts. I recently commissioned a Russian scholar to do a literal translation of a play I wanted to direct, *Artists and Admirers*, by the nineteenth-century playwright Alexander Ostrovsky, because the language in the only published translation was so inaccessible that the plot itself was unclear. She produced a version of the play that, while not colloquial, called attention to multiple meanings and idiomatic expressions. With her translation as my guide, I then adapted the language to be spoken in a more naturally conversational form.

If adapting a translation seems to take the original play too lightly, it's useful to recognize that all translations, no matter how apparently faithful, are *versions* of the original. The distance in time between a play's origin and its translation ensures that there can never be an exact correspondence. In two translations of the same play, language is not the only element that will differ. Because a translator cannot render every nuance of every word unless she creates a text many times longer than the original, certain situations and actions will unavoidably be stressed or deemphasized. The playwright and translator David Hare goes so far as to define a translation as a critique of a play:

> It's a tilt on a play . . . a matter of whether you want consciously or unconsciously to accept the fact that you are

pointing up certain parts of that play and putting others in
the shadow . . . Translators are extremely conscious of the la-
bel given to their finished product, designed to serve both as
an indicator to audience and critics of the nature of the
beast, and, naturally enough, to give due recognition to their
own level of contribution.

Often the words "adaptation" or "a version by" denote a work that has
taken greater liberties than a typical translation would. Ideally, the
particular circumstances of a single production will inform the translation. Hare's version of Brecht's *Galileo*, by his own admission, attempted to dispense with the play's German epic style of the 1950s in
order to arrive at a version suitable for London's Almeida Theatre, an
intimate venue with no wing space or system for flying in scenery.

More radical adaptations can become entirely new plays. In
Nora, his ingenious version of *A Doll's House*, Ingmar Bergman adheres to the language of the play's standard translations, yet merely by
cutting the text (and reenvisioning the final settings), he fashions a
new story with somewhat different characters. Krogstad, who lends
Nora the money she secretly uses to pay for her husband's much-
needed vacation, is transformed from a disreputable opportunist into
a sadly sympathetic victim of a past mistake. This also reduces the
play's potentially melodramatic aspects. Stylistically, *Nora* is very different from *A Doll's House*. Scenes begin and end without the ma-
chinery of realism—its carefully contrived entrances and exits. For
Ibsen's fully detailed interiors, Bergman substitutes a central platform
representing Nora's world, around which actors wait to enter as if so
bidden by her consciousness—one that is troubled from the opening
moments. Out of a realistic play, Bergman has constructed an expressionist work with the seamlessness of a dream. And he has mitigated one of the most difficult problems of *A Doll's House*—Nora's
prodigious journey from a naïve dependence on her husband to her
need to break free of their conventional marriage—by establishing a
struggle within Nora from the very beginning of the play.

RESEARCH

Not all directors do research. Some feel it inhibits their creativity; others assign it to an assistant or a dramaturg. But for most directors, research is an important phase of pre-production. "I do about six months of advance research," states Zelda Fichandler, founder of Arena Stage, "because knowledge releases my imagination. Imagination is what is there after you know everything; without knowledge, one's imagination may be too thin—lacking in strength and too fragile to build on. I need to know exactly how the characters in the play live their daily lives."

It's easy, however, for a director to become too dependent on research, allowing it to dictate not only the production approach but also the micro–acting choices in each scene. One student production of Pierre Marivaux's *The Triumph of Love* was marred because the director became absorbed with the fact that the play was originally performed in the eighteenth century by a troupe of commedia dell'arte actors. Employing farce to the exclusion of emotional reality, the production missed one of Marivaux's contributions to playwriting—a detailed exploration of the emotional repercussions of conventional comic situations.

Research will often inform my early readings of the play and the design of the production. But no matter how much background I've accumulated, I try to check most of it at the door to the rehearsal hall. Once rehearsals begin, the work with the actors, not the research, becomes the primary ingredient in directing.

There are two basic ways in which research can be valuable. It can illuminate the action, and it can guide the director in formulating the world of the play and, ultimately, the production approach. *The Glass Menagerie* is not rooted in specific historical events of the 1930s, but it is vital for the actors and director to be aware of the family's financial pressures and Depression mentality. If, from their contemporary perspective, the actors regard Laura's lack of marriage prospects as a less-than-difficult problem for the family, research into their social and economic reality could help heighten their concern.

It might also deepen their understanding of the chasm created when the children's father left home.

Altering a play's time and setting requires substantial research in both the new and the original eras, even if, as with Shakespeare, the original setting is not very detailed. Shakespeare was more interested in relating the action of a play to his own world than in creating a realistically accurate setting. Yet a director of *Macbeth, The Merchant of Venice,* or *Romeo and Juliet* should know why Shakespeare chose his settings, and how, for example, the English perceived the Scots and the Italians. The same proviso applies to Bertolt Brecht, who was not terribly concerned about geographical accuracy. Brecht, however, could not have written *In the Jungle of Cities* without having read Upton Sinclair's 1906 novel *The Jungle,* depicting the grim life of the Chicago stockyards. Knowing and reading what Brecht read would be essential for directing his play.

TYPES OF RESEARCH

There are five basic kinds of research a director can engage in. The most obvious is becoming familiar with the oeuvre of the playwright. Plays by a single writer often share a similar language, behavior, socioeconomic environment, and point of view. The most direct way of becoming acquainted with a writer is to read as many of his plays as possible. Knowing the writer's strategies and predilections will nearly always deepen a director's understanding of a single play. Diaries, sketches, letters, and other prose are often revealing. But a note of caution: a playwright's theoretical writings (like Brecht's) are not always easily applied to the plays themselves.

At a theater with a considerable staff, a dramaturg may act as the point person for researching the play, the period, and the extant translations. (An assistant director can serve the same function.) In Europe the dramaturg is a highly respected member of many theaters. As a production approach is evolved, he will often help analyze the script, flesh out the world of the play, and act as a sounding board for the director and designers. Even when a dramaturg is available, however, many directors find that doing their own research is an effective way into imagining the physical life of a play.

Period research can help identify specific references and illuminate the economic and sociopolitical outlook of the time. Since one of the director's responsibilities is to help the actors create behavior, knowledge of a period's everyday life is always useful. Fortunately, there's been a recent increase in such historical studies. One example is the marvelously titled *What Jane Austen Ate and Charles Dickens Knew: From Fox Hunting to Whist—the Facts of Daily Life in 19th-Century England*, which covers the social gamut from dinner parties to grave robbing. For a recent production of Philip Barry's *Holiday*, an urbane romantic comedy set in late 1920s America, a dramaturg produced a packet of readings for the director and actors, consisting of articles on manners, courtship, parenting, and travel. Like many directors, I dip into the art and music of a play's world to

TIP: AMERICAN RESEARCH

Many new and extraordinary research tools have become available in the last decade or so, such as the Internet and superb CD-ROMs like *The American Century*, an offbeat pictorial history of social trends. But these tools should not discourage the director from seeking less obvious material. One of my favorite low-tech sources for early- and mid-twentieth-century plays is the Sears, Roebuck and Company catalog. Sears made an extraordinary range of products in that era, so the catalog is a treasure trove of Americana. Its descriptions of most of the objects found in U.S. households is a Rosetta stone for the behavior of the time. When I directed *The Glass Menagerie* in Tokyo, the 1935 catalog was an invaluable tool for familiarizing the designers with the world of the play.

help articulate a production style. Ideally, period research should promote an elaborate, ambiguous, and contradictory appreciation of that world, much like that of our own.

Every well-known playwright is the subject of biographical and critical work, a third category of research. As with all other research, the director must cull to find truly useful material. When I directed *Nora*, I came across a book of essays called *Ibsen's Heroines*, which examined many of the playwright's characters. Although published in the 1920s, the descriptions seemed surprisingly acute and contemporary. (I later learned that the author, Lou Salomé, was a female psychoanalyst and friend of Freud's.) Torvald, Nora's husband, was described as "a conventional pained person, saturated with fear" whose "delight in simple gaiety and loveliness is a conventional person's reluctance to face any struggle." For myself and Michael York, who played Torvald, this one sentence was the key that unlocked the role, revealing Torvald as deeply flawed but profoundly sympathetic. It explained his love for Nora, his conventional views, and his cowardice. It even suggested why Rank, his good friend, refuses to allow Torvald to attend him during his final struggle with illness and death.

Much of today's literary criticism is highly academic, designed to peddle theories rather than elucidate works of literature, and thus is of little use in directorial research. This wasn't always the case. For example, Jan Kott's *Shakespeare Our Contemporary* has had a remarkable influence on Shakespeare productions, including those of Peter Brook. With persistence, one can uncover books that provide penetrating insight into character and narrative structure.

Directors are divided on the benefit of a fourth type of research—a play's production history. Some are concerned about being unduly influenced by previous productions, but I think ignoring important past productions would be naïve and disengaged from theatrical history. The acclaimed director André Serban, well known for his intense research into a play's production history, claims it allows him to steal the best ideas and meld them into a "ratatouille" of his own. As he attempts to make plays seem fresh, his productions consciously critique the habits and clichés of past productions. I once saw Serban rifle through pages of production photographs in *Theater Heute*, a German theater magazine, pilfering images that appealed to him. Directors, like writers, are scavengers. We use a myriad of sources to find inspiration. As I'll describe in Chapter 5, a production of Ferenc Molnár's *The Guardsman* that I directed was greatly influenced, in a contrary way, by a photograph of the original New York production.

Perhaps the most valuable source for production research is the vast collection at the Lincoln Center Library for the Performing Arts in New York City. Nearly every produced play has a file, with copies of national and local reviews, press clippings, and feature articles. In addition, there may be original programs and promptbooks, set designs, and photographs. Reviews can be instructive when they point to difficulties in the text and challenges for productions.

Most directors find it essential to share some of their research with the cast. Without some background to stimulate the exploration of behavior, rehearsals of a period play usually feel hollow. One recent trend has been to encourage the actors to embrace their initial impressions of the period or culture, no matter how clichéd. In rehearsing a Chekhov play, for instance, actors might be asked to improvise scenes without research, based on their ideas of "what is Russian." These types of exercises might benefit very ironic texts in the earliest stages of rehearsal, but they will be of limited value for a play of any depth.

A fifth type of research utilized by some directors borrows from the more specific and informed tradition of England's protean Joint Stock Company, which routinely went into the field to research the lives of ordinary people during the first weeks of rehearsals. The actors would reassemble and use their findings to interview one another and ultimately to provide a playwright with the foundation for a text. This was exactly the method adopted by the Tectonic Theatre Company in developing *The Laramie Project*, a play, written by company members, that explored in minute detail the murder of Matthew Shepard, a young gay man in a small Wyoming town. Under the guidance and initiative of the company's founder, Moises Kaufman, the actors made numerous trips to Laramie, interviewing a remarkable range of the town's citizens. In performance, the impact of their shared research was powerfully evident. While such commitment is not the norm, sharing and discussing selective research can fire and embolden the imagination, inspiring a cast to inhabit their roles and depend on one another. Part of the joy of directing is exploring new worlds, and research can be a first step in that exploration.

THREE

INTERPRETING THE ACTION

For some directors, interpreting a play consists entirely of working with actors in rehearsal. For others, like myself, starting that process without extensive preparation would be like conducting a laboratory experiment without a hypothesis. The interpretive work that a director does in pre-production is of course conjectural, but it's also, to my mind, an essential passageway into rehearsals.

Interpretation rarely proceeds in an organized fashion. You might have an understanding of the structure of a play before discovering the primary goals of the characters. Or the genesis of a unifying idea for the physical production may take shape before you've done a thorough structural analysis. In order to display an entire interpretive process, I've separated and ordered the various stages here. This chapter and the two that follow form an inductive approach to interpretation, starting with *action* (or internal) analysis, then moving to *structural* (external) analysis, and finally to the formulation of an *approach* for the entire play. This order reflects my preference for working from the specific to the general. How internal interpretation is put into practice is the subject of Chapter 9, a companion to this chapter.

Unfortunately, many theaters require that the set and costume design on a production be completed long before actors arrive. This means that it's especially important to work intensively on the text before collaborating with designers. Without preparation, it's all too easy to fix on a concept (a unifying idea, which I prefer to call an *approach*) before developing an in-depth understanding of a play. So it is not uncommon to hear directors float far-fetched ideas such as "Let's set *King Lear* on the moon" or "Here's a concept: *The Taming of the Shrew* in the Old West" or "We'll turn it into a musical, with a live band and production numbers." A concept arrived at with little intensive exploration and research is more likely to conflict with a text than illuminate it. This chapter recommends that the director begin the interpretive process by breaking the script down into units of action.

Since plays are webs of intentional behavior, action, *the physical pursuit of a goal or desire*, is the constant—and, for most actors and directors, the clearest way into a text. Actions are the internal mechanism or engine of a play, and identifying them is critical both to shaping an approach to the play and to directing the actors. Once you decipher actions for the scenes, overall actions (or objectives) for the entire play will emerge. If you formulate them effectively, the objectives of the two main characters (or groups of characters) will constitute a central conflict, the key to telling the story and imparting the ideas. For Vsevolod Meyerhold, one of the great directors of the last century, words were merely "decorations on the skirts of actions." It is hardly surprising that the director is often referred to as the "author of the action."

TIP: TERMINOLOGY

Many directors use similar terminology when working with actors, though the exact meanings that they apply to the terms vary widely. I use *action*, which includes both desire and its physical pursuit, to identify the behavior of characters attempting to achieve their goals within a scene. Sometimes *action* and *objective* are employed synonymously, though I prefer to think of *objective* as denoting the umbrella under which all of the actions of a scene should fit. (*Activity*—specific physical tasks, such as lighting a cigarette or setting a table—should not be confused with *action*, which is a more comprehensive term that involves an intention. Even when there is no activity in a scene, there is still action).

Highlighting action exposes the *subtext*, the underlying meaning and action of the dialogue. In realistic plays, the dialogue and the subtext are often at odds with each other; characters say one thing but mean something else. But with more highly styled plays, such as Shakespeare's, the subtext is limited because the text itself spells out action and meaning more directly.

Action is the motor of a story and its connecting tissue, but it isn't always apparent in the dialogue. Often it has to be teased out. In Chekhov's plays, the dialogue is actually a screen for the action—which usually becomes apparent only by identifying the subtext.

NAMING THE ACTION

Action is most effectively understood and communicated as a transitive verb in the formula *Character x ———s character y* (or *Character x is———ing character y*). For example, the action of one scene might be that character x *commands* character y to tell the truth, while y *flatters* x in an attempt to avoid answering x. In another scene, x might *threaten* y, who then, in response, finds a way to *sabotage* x. Using intransitive verbs (*Character x is angry about y*) often promotes playing a condition or state of being instead of an action, and asking

an actor to play a state of being more often than not produces generalized and artificial acting. Sometimes it may seems as if a character
plays an action to or for himself, or for his own sake (as in a soliloquy). But that action will eventually be used to affect another character.

TIP: REFINING THE ACTION

Determining the characters' actions in a scene and communicating them effectively are two of the most critical
practices—more intuitive and visceral than intellectual—
for a director to learn. If you find it difficult to define the
action of a scene, first ask what the character is *literally* doing. Then consider the objective behind that behavior. For
instance, if character x is literally questioning character y, is
he *badgering* her, *testing* her, or *searching* for an answer?
An aid in identifying action is to read all of a single character's lines in that scene or smaller unit consecutively. This
gives you a better chance to sense how the lines connect to
form an action and how the character's several actions become the tactics for achieving an objective.

When stating the characters' actions doesn't help clarify a scene, it's often because the wrong actions have been
chosen—they don't express the character's desires. When I
can't sense a viable action, I try to ascertain what character
x wants from character y, instead of just testing verb after
verb. When you become specific about what a character
wants in relation to another character, actable verbs
emerge. Even experienced actors and directors have to remind themselves that characters are always trying to get
something from each other.

BEATS

Every change of action produces a new segment, called a *beat*, which is often defined as "a single unit of action." (A beat, for directors and actors, is very different from a pause, but playwrights sometimes use the word to indicate one.) Breaking down a script into beats makes it possible for actors and directors to work with units smaller than a scene and to clarify the characters' changes. Segmenting the scenes gives you a much better chance of communicating the story to an audience. Determining exactly where and how a beat changes is a key matter of interpretation in a rehearsal process. And attempting to define a single action for each character in each beat is one of the best ways for a director to prepare for rehearsals. Some teachers and textbooks advocate listing an action for every line, a practice I find tedious and confusing. For actors, working with a director who stopped to give a different action for each line would be excruciating. Focusing mostly on the beat rather than on the line allows the actor the freedom to make her own contribution to the process.

TIP: BEAT CHANGES

Playwrights often provide clues for detecting where a new beat begins. Some do it with a stage direction, though not all stage directions indicate a beat change. A pause very often marks a beat change, as does a discovery or the entrance of a new character. But a character can change the subject while still playing the same action. Since a beat change often indicates a change in rhythm, the scene breakdown also highlights the play's changing patterns of rhythm and tempo.

Once you start formally analyzing the text, take notes for each scene on the actions and their context—the *given circumstances*. A

common practice is to place a blank page opposite each page of dialogue, divide it into columns representing "actions" and "obstacles,"
and make notes within them for each beat. This helps disclose how
the action changes, ebbs, and flows. When I make notes, it has to be
in pencil, since my ideas are exploratory, tentative, and likely to
change again and again before and during rehearsals.

GIVEN CIRCUMSTANCES

Determining a character's action can be done only while simultaneously considering the given circumstances, which are often the cata-
lysts that propel the character into action. "Givens" incorporate all
the background and present conditions of a character's world, from
the scene's setting to the previous action. Each character has his or
her own set of given circumstances, some of which, such as the setting, they share with other characters. In *The Glass Menagerie*, the
hivelike Wingfield apartment, one of many "cellular living-units . . .
in over-crowded urban centers," is a given circumstance for all the
characters in the play, though its effect on each character will be different. Amanda sees it, however threadbare, as the family home;
Laura finds solace in it; Tom eventually has to escape it.

Realistic plays tend to be extremely rich in the given circumstances that are spelled out in the text, which is one of the reasons for
using a play like *The Glass Menagerie* to illustrate them. The second
scene of Act 1 (found in Appendix Three, page 213) contains considerable previous action, though only one scene has preceded it. Laura
has stayed away from Rubicam's Business College ever since she
broke down during a speed typing test. She has spent her days at the
zoo, the art museum, and the movies. Amanda returns home after a
humiliating visit to the college, where a teacher dispelled her assumption that Laura had been attending class. Longer-term circumstances also serve to charge the scene and instigate action. With her
husband having run off, Amanda has had to worry about the financial condition of the family. Her concern grows out of an awareness
of Laura's shyness, her limp, and her limited prospects in business

and marriage. Any realistic scene has numerous given circumstances, but usually one or two immediate ones will predominate. In this scene, it is Amanda's mortifying experience at the college.

Less realistic plays, such as those of Shakespeare, Molière, the Greeks, and many others, require actors and directors to invent given circumstances in addition to those mentioned in the text in order to connect and give context to the characters' actions. Yet no play, no matter how realistic, lays out every possible given circumstance. One of the charges of the director and actors is to imagine and test out circumstances that fill in where the script leaves off. The *motivation* for a character's action is often to be found in the given circumstances: for example, Amanda's visit to the college is all the inducement she needs to confront Laura with the truth.

UNCOVERING THE ACTION

At the top of the second scene, Laura is discovered listening to a record and polishing her glass collection, having skipped typing class. When she hears the key rattle in the lock, she crosses guiltily to the typewriter. Amanda enters with a stricken expression on her face, and Laura pretends to type. Her charade is shaken by Amanda's detailed account of the visit to Rubicam's. Laura admits she has left school, and Amanda asks difficult questions about their future. She settles on marriage as the only course for Laura and inquires about any past interest in men that Laura might have had. Laura mentions a boy in high school whom she admired, which inspires Amanda to start planning Laura's future. She minimizes Laura's handicap with a lesson about the value of charm.

This is what literally happens in the scene. The director's next step is to find the essential actions for each character, describe them in strong, compelling terms, and note where they change. You'll need to be patient and attentive to detail in order to recognize all the beats. The first beat is very short—it involves only Laura, as she listens to music and tends to the menagerie. If Laura's action in this first beat—and perhaps others—is to *relish favorite pastimes*, the scene will play quite differently than if it were *killing time*. (The latter choice of action might paint Laura as too helpless.)

Once she hears Amanda's arrival, Laura abruptly changes her action, moving to the typewriter to *fabricate an air of normality*. In this beat, we might define Amanda's action as *getting Laura's attention* or *destroying the charade* by tearing up her typing charts and demanding that she acknowledge her age. The beat probably ends when the pressure of the guilt applied by Amanda is too much for Laura to bear. Not coincidentally, Williams inserts a pause at this point, followed by Amanda's direct, heartfelt cry, "What are we going to do?" During that pause, the actress playing Laura probably can't go on typing or pretending that nothing is wrong; she has to respond to her mother's actions.

I noted a "probable" spot for this beat change, because productions will differ about the choice of actions and when they change. If you marked a third beat when Amanda tore up the typing charts, you would not be alone. But if, in that second beat, Amanda's action was defined as *destroying her charade*, might not tearing up the charts be part of that action? In fact, the next line, Laura's "Why did you do that, Mother" does seem to continue the pretense she adopted when Amanda appeared.

As I mentioned, deciding where to mark a beat is always interpretive, some changes of action being more obvious than others. Deciding exactly on what line a beat changes may seem insignificant, but eventually it affects the way the actors play the scene and how the story is told. Having too many beat changes might make the action less clear, less fluid, and finally harder for the audience to read.

After doing this analysis for some time, you'll notice that a beat always marks a change in the actions of *both* characters. This is because a new action played by one character forces a new response in the other. Can a character return to an action played in a previous beat? Perhaps, but if the actions in all of a scene's beats are different, it'll be much easier to get the actors to understand and play the scene's progression.

Is there another beat change in the pause that occurs after

Amanda's "What is the future?" Possibly. But it could also be that the same beat that starts with "What are we going to do" plays through the entire story of Amanda's visit to the college. Her action in that long beat could be articulated as *pleading with Laura to face reality*. It should be obvious that the beat would play very differently were we to choose an action such as Amanda *berates Laura for lying*.

Laura's reaction to the story of her mother's experience at the college is to burrow back inside herself, retreating to the phonograph. Amanda reacts by scolding her—"Oh don't *do* that, Laura!"—and Laura is taken aback. This begins a new beat, in which we might say she *confronts Laura with the lie*, and this beat plays through Laura's agony at the suffering look on her mother's face. While Amanda is confronting her, Laura *counters her mother's disappointment* (or *proves she has a satisfying life*) with an account of her enjoyable visits to the zoo, the museum, and the movies. The next beat might begin with Amanda's challenge to Laura, "So what are we going to do now, honey?" with her action being to *persuade Laura that marriage is her best hope*. The following beat has Amanda *eliciting Laura's story* about the crush she had on a high school boy. And the last very short beat, a tender one, comprises Amanda *encouraging Laura to think positively* rather than dwell on her defect.

By working with actions and beats, we've discovered that the scene begins with a distraught Amanda feeling hopeless about Laura's future and concludes with the mother encouraging the daughter to think of herself as a charming catch for a suitor. This may not seem exceptional, yet a surprising number of readers would cite the scene as evidence that Amanda is a manipulative shrew—a characterization that does not square with the action. Examining the beat structure and its progression helps to develop the characters, not by generalizing about their personalities, but by discovering what they do. In pre-production you need not be overly concerned with the exact wording of actions or the placement of beats, but whatever work you can do will help you see more possibilities once rehearsals begin.

SCENE OBJECTIVES

Because a playwright writes the dialogue of a scene as a complete unit, each scene has an essential wholeness that can be expressed by a *scene objective*, which serves as a check on the actions of the scene. If we looked at what happens in scene 2 as a whole, we might describe Amanda's objective as *awakening Laura to take action to secure her future*. Both criticism and encouragement fit within that objective, so we are probably on the right track. Everything Laura does in the scene is meant to *defuse her mother's anger and disappointment*. This includes actions as diverse as playing the phonograph, sharing her outings, and telling of her crush on Jim O'Connor. Even her pretense at the beginning of the scene can be interpreted as *puncturing the air of doom* that Amanda's entrance creates. It's easy to pay less attention to the needs of the follower, but again, if Laura's actions are neglected, she may seem morose and victimized.

If the exploration of action is the center of the director's work, it's also the most difficult aspect to master. Although the only way that determining actions can become second nature is to test it out in your directing, one simple way to increase your understanding of actions and objectives is to examine everyday behavior in those terms. When a friend stops at your house unexpectedly, it's natural to wonder what his purpose—or *objective*—might be. If he compliments your interior decoration, praises your wife, and complains about being strapped for cash, you'll probably conclude he is there *to plead for a loan*. When he makes the request, you can look back and realize that actions such as praising your wife and home, while seemingly not connected to asking for a loan, were in fact part of that objective.

OBSTACLES: THE FLIP SIDE OF ACTIONS

In attempting to achieve their goals, characters face *obstacles*. Without obstacles, they would fulfill their every desire, and plays would be happy and short. An obstacle acts as a hard, resistant surface to the knife of action; it can brake, deter, or stimulate a character. Like the grinding of a knife against a stone, the friction between action and obstacle produces sparks and heightens conflict.

Imagine a scene in a crowded ballroom. A young man has just caught sight of his girlfriend across the room. Not surprisingly, his objective is *to join his love*. To achieve this objective, he must fight his way through the crowd, avoiding large groups, waving to acquaintances to forestall conversations, and apologizing to those he runs into. These obstacles force him to work harder to achieve his goal, making his journey more dramatic. If the ballroom were only half full, his objective would be easily accomplished and a lot less interesting.

Amanda's objective of awakening Laura to the need to secure her future, with all its subordinate actions, faces many obstacles, most of which are represented by Laura. She is shy, reclusive, and unskilled. She spends much of her time listening dreamily to music and polishing her glass collection. She suffers from a disability that she sees as an enormous affliction. And she has little incentive to think about her future. Laura's objective of defusing her mother's anger has its own obstacles, including Amanda's humiliation at the college and her reaction to finding that Laura has left school.

There are also obstacles within each character that make achieving their objectives difficult. The shame Amanda felt at the college makes it harder for her to awaken Laura to her future. Another obstacle is her fear, having heard the story of Laura's breakdown, that Laura may not have the strength to overcome her isolation. In plays of consistently direct conflict, such as those of David Mamet, internal obstacles play a less important role; the obstacles for each character lie in the other characters. But in most plays, ignoring internal obstacles usually produces acting that lacks the variety, interest, and drama created by internal struggle.

PUTTING ACTIONS AND OBSTACLES TOGETHER

In the opening scene of *Nora* (see page 219), Ingmar Bergman has distilled the first scene of *A Doll's House* into a discussion about money between Nora and her husband Torvald. Nora invites him to take a look at the packages she purchased that surround the Christmas tree; he lectures her on thrift and then offers to buy her a Christmas present. She begs Torvald for cash, which she needs in order to help pay off the loan she has kept secret from him. He puts her off by starting to leave. She then brings their discussion back to an easier subject—inviting a friend to a Christmas celebration. This apparently talky domestic scene is actually packed with actions that form a tense, complex subtext.

At the top of the scene, Nora *coaxes Torvald to pay attention* by mentioning her purchases. At first he *tries to ignore her,* but the beat seems to change as early as the middle of his first line, when Nora's mention of purchases catches his ear. She then tries *teasing more money out of Torvald.* He responds by *cautioning her on their finances.* Marking the point where he takes out his wallet as the end of the beat would not be surprising. My initial impulse, however, would be to start the third beat well before that point, after Nora says, "We'll borrow in the meantime," since the very suggestion causes Torvald to begin a new action—*preaching the evils of borrowing.* Nora attempts to *get Torvald back on the right track* by accepting his lecture, and her acquiescence prompts him to *entice* her with a small amount of cash to abandon the plan for an extravagant Christmas. She takes the money but *begs* for a Christmas present in cash, causing Torvald to *remind her of her spendthrift ways.* Interestingly, though hurt by his remarks, she *pulls him back into the holiday spirit,* by making sure he has invited their friend Dr. Rank to dinner. For the time being, Nora retreats from a losing position, and Torvald kisses her to *celebrate the good fortune* of his promotion to bank manager.

By working with actions, we have found that the very first scene of the play, an apparently innocent domestic encounter that ends in a kiss, is actually a tightly contested power struggle. On that basis, we could conclude that Nora's scene objective is *to loosen the miser,* an objective that includes actions like flirting, begging, and cajoling. Torvald's actions seem to add up to an objective of *restraining Nora's extravagance.* He does this through actions such as administering rationality, lecturing her on borrowing, and tendering a bribe—all in order to control what he considers to be her profligate ways.

One of the benefits of this work is that we can now see the basic physics of the scene: how action produces reaction, how cause produces effect, and how action and obstacle are linked. The conflict within the *Nora* scene is clear and direct, and the actions of one character serve as the obstacles for the other. Her greatest external obstacle is his parsimony. His major obstacle is her supposed extravagance. Notice how the given circumstances heighten the obstacles and the need for further actions. Torvald's recent promotion to bank manager means that Nora will see him as well-off and ask for even more money. The setting of the scene close to Christmas gives Nora a chance to accumulate a bit more money to pay off her debt. Her recent shopping trip is the most immediate, pressing, and useful given circumstance, charging the scene with even more urgency.

The work of this chapter, articulating actions and obstacles, is as much a matter of empathy as intellect. As the process evolves and deepens, it must be fed increasingly by the imagination. To fully understand the choices actors make, a director must intimately engage with the circumstances of the play. Why does Torvald fear Nora's extravagance? How does she feel about having the debt? Why does she need more than the usual allowance from her husband? Is it just a matter of paying off her lender, or is it tied to a deeper sense of pride and dignity? In *The Glass Menagerie*, what is it about Amanda's doomed expression that makes Laura share her adventures at the zoo with her? What makes Laura stay home most of the time? What does her day consist of? A perennial question to ask is, What are the circumstances that compel the characters to perform their actions?

Breaking down scenes by action raises many of the questions that will come up in rehearsals and begins the process of exploring what happens in each scene. Preparing the scenes should be a stimulus for the director, not a diagram. As clever as this work may seem on the page, the director must be ready to toss it all away if rehearsal discoveries prove more useful.

THE RATIONALE BEHIND ACTION

Konstantin Stanislavski revolutionized modern theater by observing the best actors of his time and concluding that to play honestly, an actor cannot normally approach emotion directly. Authentic emotion arises, he found, as a by-product of doing something else—of pursuing a goal, of playing an action. With the great majority of actors, concentrating on portraying emotion directly is a prescription for *indicating*—which is when an actor illustrates emotions rather than playing action.

Recently it has become fashionable to blame Stanislavski for everything from the excesses of the Method to the psychological bent of much of American theater. But those who dismiss his contributions as nothing more than the seeds of one strain of American acting fail to take into account the body of his work. One of the supreme ironies in the development of American acting technique is that at the time when the Method emerged, only the first of Stanislavki's three books had been translated into English. While Lee Strasberg claimed to have invented a Stanislavskian acting Method that emphasized emotional memory and self-analysis, he was aware only of *An Actor Prepares*, which stresses the importance of the actor's personal connection to a role. Despite objections from those who had studied with Stanislavski himself and knew his work—such as Stella Adler—the Method, and with it much of American acting, maintained this narrow focus, largely ignoring the other two books. In *Building a Character* and *Creating a Role*, Stanislavski balanced the physical and the emotional, promoting a way for actors to work from the inside out *and* from the outside in. In fact, it may well have been Stanislavski who spawned many of the twentieth century's physical acting techniques. Another irony: some Method actors became so caught up in emotionalizing that they were incapable of doing what all of Stanislavski's work emphasized—playing action!

Though he arrived at some of the same conclusions that Freud did, Stanislavski did not introduce psychology into theater practice. In order to communicate the extraordinary perceptions of some of history's greatest playwrights, most notably Shakespeare, actors through the ages have had to understand and embody the intricacies of human emotion. If many of the insights produced by the process described in this chapter have been psychological, it's because psychology is an important factor in realistic plays. The process of exploring action isn't inherently psychological; it doesn't favor a particular style or aesthetic. Searching for and playing actions is just as useful with Shakespeare and produces more than psychological insights. The part of the interpretative process represented by this chapter is, in fact, one way of doing what most successful directors do—entering the imagination of the playwright and preparing to direct the actor by determining how goals are pursued. The director who ignores the emotional life of each character, focusing entirely on gesture and movement, risks diminishing the imagination of virtually any play, regardless of its style.

FOUR

EXTERNAL ANALYSIS: STRUCTURE

To some extent, the preparation for directors outlined in the last chapter overlaps the work of actors. This chapter balances the internal interpretation of characters' desires with the external analysis of dramatic structure. Very often a director and cast will find themselves unsure of or in disagreement over the actions of a scene. One way to test an action is to measure it against the play's formal properties, its overall structure.

CENTRAL CONFLICT: THE DIRECTORIAL HANDLE

As actions and scene objectives accumulate, the characters' desires for the entire play, often called *superobjectives*, come into focus. A hunch about them might occur early on, especially to the experienced director, but it's more likely to arise out of the intensive work of breaking scenes down. Employing the term *superobjective* in coaching actors can produce too much thinking, but the director herself should know how a character's actions add up to create one major desire. Recognizing these overall wants allows a director to structure the entire play by activating a *central conflict*—x's objective versus y's—forming a bridge between the internal and external, between actions and structure. Good drama—and comedy—is always characterized by strong conflict. In terms of simple physics, conflict creates tension, struggle, friction, and energy. Direct conflict increases energy exponentially. Even if the central conflict is not as direct as, for instance, x and y both wanting the deed to the family home, you can usually restate the superobjectives to create a more forceful collision.

Most plays, even those with many characters, are built around a protagonist and an antagonist (or occasionally two opposing groups of characters), and the rest of the characters tend to line up on one side of the conflict or the other. Since the central conflict also carries a play's conflict of ideas, it expresses, more specifically than the themes, the principal subjects of the play. Thousands of plays contain the theme of the family or the theme of youth, so starting our analysis by hunting for themes doesn't take us much below the surface. *The Glass Menagerie* contains many themes, but it is constructed around a single conflict: Amanda versus Tom, loyalty versus the individual needs of the emerging artist. Not all conflicts are as clear as that of *The Glass Menagerie*. Different productions of the same play often reflect the constructing of different central conflicts.

Setting up the central conflict is one of a director's most useful strategies. The struggle between the major contending forces is the crux of the story and an ideal springboard for designing the play's physical world. Identifying the central conflict is the director's most effective overarching tool for both preparation and rehearsals.

FUNCTION

Every element of a story has a purpose or *function*, and once you've settled on a central conflict, it's much easier to establish the function of each character and narrative element. In order to tell a story effectively, the director—as the person responsible for the way the events unfurl—must know the function of each part in order to determine how best to fulfill it.

It's not enough to say that the function of a scene is to develop the characters, because all well-written scenes do that. In analyzing a scene's function, try to specify the aspects of plot and relationship that occur within the scene. The second scene of *The Glass Menagerie* exposes Laura's lie about going to school. But it also brings about a new understanding between the two characters that they must now pay attention to changing Laura's inertia. Without that understanding, further action couldn't proceed, since there'd be little reason for Amanda to coax Tom into bringing home a date for his sister. Scene 2 also sketches Laura's dependence on her mother and the love Amanda feels for her daughter. (The scene is not about Amanda punishing Laura, though surprisingly it is sometimes played that way.) If the characters never demonstrate that love, the actions and objectives of the scene need to be reworked. An understanding of function provides a framework for making decisions on characters' actions.

The opening scene of *Nora* is the first demonstration of the struggle for control that characterizes the marriage of Nora and Torvald. He's in command, but she has ways of pulling the strings. The scene establishes his paternalism and Nora's frequent acquiescence. It also illustrates the couple's flirtatious affection. If both elements aren't in the playing, the scene will be one-dimensional and unsurprising.

A function of all scenes is to convey information, and a director and actors who identify and highlight the initial mention of critical information will give the audience a much better chance of appreciating the story. (See "The Watergate Question" in Chapter 11.) A director must be aware of the ways a playwright unfolds character, plot, and relationship to be able to support those strategies. Without this awareness, an audience will be confused because moments of revelation will probably not receive the emphasis and clarity they need.

EVENT

Related to a scene's function is its *event*. Every play is a series of events. We could conceivably call every speech or interchange between characters an event. But for most directors, the term encompasses all the incidents of a scene or an entire play. We might think of the event of the first scene from *Nora* as her *attempt to use the holiday to extract more money from Torvald*, because everything Nora does—as well as Torvald's reactions—is contained in that statement. The event concludes in a stalemate, with Torvald offering Nora a present but not the cash Christmas gift she prefers. Bergman pared down the first scene of *A Doll's House* to just this particular event to emphasize that both characters are involved in acts of extortion. This, Bergman wants us to immediately note, is what to a great extent defines their marriage. Various directors will identify different events and thus produce different interpretations. When you identify the event, it becomes much easier to determine actions, and when actions and event are in harmony, the interpretation is likely to be clear and consistent.

The event of the *Glass Menagerie* scene might be *realizing the need to take action to secure Laura's future*. This event begins with the very first confrontational beats and continues through the plan at the very end of the scene. Like function, event is another way of creating an external barometer against which actions can be tested. If Amanda loses faith in Laura or punishes her, the event I've cited will be derailed. And if playing the scene doesn't accomplish the event, the actions are inappropriate.

In interpreting an entire play, events are far more useful than subjects or themes, because events are the building blocks of a play's structure. Some directors use the term *central action* instead of *event*. Gregory Mosher, who directed some of David Mamet's early plays, distinguishes between the *action* of *American Buffalo* and its *subject*: "I asked David, 'What is the subject of the play?' He said, 'Honor among thieves.' And that's true. I believe that is the subject of the play, but it's not the action of the play." Mosher cites the central action (or event) of the entire play as "the destruction of a relationship between a father and son." He adds that a director focusing on the robbery rather than the relationship would set the play off on a wrong course.

Establishing a play's event is more than an abstract exercise. Even in a play like Samuel Beckett's *Krapp's Last Tape*, in which an old man does little more than install and listen to a tape recording, there is still action and event. A director describing the play's event as *attempting to bring back the past* or *escaping into the past to hide from present pain* would probably create a more nostalgic production than a director who defined the event as *preparing for death by summing up one's life*.

ARCHITECTURE

Yet another important external characteristic of a scene is *architecture*. By this I mean the way a scene develops. To understand how most scenes are structured, let's consider a single speech: Amanda's tale of woe at Rubicam's Business College. The first beat of the speech is a recounting of an argument between Amanda and the typing instructor about whether Laura has been a student at the school, with the instructor unable to remember Laura. Amanda's repeated assertions that Laura has been attending classes set up her eventual humiliation. From the function of this *rising action*, you can see that if Amanda is somewhat vehement in her assertions, her eventual humiliation will be that much greater. Then comes the concrete evidence of Laura's name and the record of her absences in the attendance book. This unit functions to deepen the irony; the audience knows Laura hasn't been attending, even as Amanda continues to insist that she has. The turning point of the story probably occurs when the teacher recalls how Laura became so ill she was unable to take the speed test. From this moment on, the story can have only one direction and conclusion—Amanda's humiliation. The climax of the story is the teacher's graphic description of Laura's breakdown.

The falling action, or denouement, consists of Amanda's acknowledgment of shame and lost hopes.

The structure of a scene—and even an entire play—is often similar to that of a single speech. In plays of all styles, there are rising actions, complications, a turning point, a climax, and falling action. Even scenes from nonlinear plays contain some, if not all, of these features. Nor is this structure limited to Western or European writing, as evidenced by many African tribal rituals and Brazilian stories of the crowning of kings. More abstract plays may not have standard climaxes, but they will have heightened moments, as well as an internal dynamic, that give structure to their stories.

When we tell a story or joke, we make instinctive use of structural elements. We may start in a casual way, trying to take the listener by surprise, while being sure to underline key information. We add complications (the rising action), which develop the story and intensify the suspense. Perhaps we pause for emphasis before uttering the climax or punch line. We then add falling action to allow the impact of the story to take hold. While actors may be aware of the dynamics of a scene, it's the director's job to orchestrate the structure in order to tell an effective story.

In our scene from *The Glass Menagerie*, the action rises through the exposure of Laura's lie and Amanda's dark speech about the awful fate of spinsters. To my mind, the scene turns with Laura's revelation of her crush on a boy. Startled by Laura's admission, Amanda responds, "You did?" It's at this turning point that Amanda senses there is hope. The scene then proceeds to her pep talk. The turning point also happens to be a beat change, supporting the assumption that this is indeed an important moment in the scene. The climax of the scene would seem to be in Amanda's last speech, when she overcomes Laura's feelings about being disabled with the advice to cultivate charm.

The turning point in the short first scene of *Nora* is highly interpretable. Is it when Torvald takes out his wallet and counts out Nora's allowance? Or could it be when he asks her to name something she'd like to have for Christmas? At the latter point, he does seem to do more than merely reward Nora for listening to his lecture on thrift. (Might his new action be to attempt to uncover Nora's plan for herself or to make sure she wants a reasonable gift?) The climax of the scene seems more apparent: his slap at Nora's inability to save, which cuts her to the quick. We know from further information in the play that she is proud of her ability to pay for the vacation that kept Torvald alive, but she resists disputing him here and revealing her secret. The falling action of the scene begins with the stage direction that indicates he "wants to leave." His gesture establishes a new beat, as Nora "keeps him in her arms" to maintain the holiday spirit.

In looking at the architecture of a scene, you'll want to pinpoint all key moments. Being aware of them enables a director to decide what to emphasize and even how to allocate rehearsal time. Your sense of the key moments of a scene becomes yet another way of testing the validity of the actions. Like the function and event of a scene, its architecture is open to interpretation. But no matter what the interpretation, if key moments are left unhighlighted, the story will be difficult for the audience to comprehend.

ARCHETYPAL PATTERNS

In addition to its architecture, a play also exhibits global patterns with which a director should be familiar. Some of Chekhov's plays, for instance, are built around social occasions, in which each act features a different ritual. An awareness of this structure can affect the way the occasions are acted and designed. Genre is an important global element in every play because playwrights are always attuned to it. Knowing the type of story you're working on makes it possible to fashion an appropriate tone and style.

One of the most imaginative and useful systems for analyzing genre was devised by Northrop Frye in *Anatomy of Criticism*, an encyclopedia of narrative strategies and the archetypal patterns that characterize them. (Unfortunately, Frye's work has gone out of fashion with contemporary literary theorists. They see his categorizations as being restrictive and out of touch with postmodernism, even though Frye steadily contends that many works of literature draw elements from more than one genre.) In his discussion of comedy, Frye identifies a pattern of many comedies as the movement from one society to another, ending in a final social ritual, usually a wedding. To create a buoyant ending, this type of comedy includes as many of the characters as possible in the final celebration. A *Midsummer Night's Dream*, with its multiple marriages, follows this pattern. Many other comedies do not, and recognizing the differences will make a play's individuality more apparent. *Twelfth Night* ends with romantic couplings but doesn't include all the characters in the festivities. The exclusion of Malvolio in the last scene is, as many modern directors have noted, a significant departure from typical romantic comedy that affects the ending and possibly the tone of the entire play.

Many plays contain strains of myth, folk, or fairy tale. Sometimes a classic story element is used without much adaptation, but more often it's transfigured in ways that highlight the individuality of the new narrative. The power of many of Shakespeare's plays often comes from the unique transformation of archetypal stories. Elements of the Cinderella tale, for instance, can be found in a number of his plays, most notably *All's Well That Ends Well*, with a ring substituting for the slipper. Part of the surprise of the play is that it is a woman, not a man, who pursues an ideal love. Even more confounding is that the naïve and callow Bertram is anything but Prince Charming. Shakespeare's take on the fairy tale points up the uniqueness of his narrative. (*All's Well* also contains a prototypical Renaissance archetype, that of the redemption occasioned by the reappearance of a virgin. Interestingly, these kinds of patterns often cross diverse cultures: the story of Cinderella appears to have had its origin in ninth-century China.) When myth, genre, and archetype are allowed to influence a production, character and story become more layered and enjoyable.

A grasp of familiar story elements also sheds light on the world of the play. For example, the typical movement of a romantic comedy, Frye maintains, is a rhythmic cycle from a normal world to a "green world" or pastoral setting and back again. *As You Like It* is a classic example that embraces this movement, while more ironic comedies such as *All's Well That Ends Well* and *Measure for Measure* do not. If you're sensitive to the consequences of narrative strategies, you will deepen your understanding of the various worlds of a play. This understanding can be of great value when you start to work with designers on imagining how to realize those worlds onstage.

What makes *The Glass Menagerie* such a bittersweet play is its poignant combination of comic, ironic, and somewhat tragic story elements. In one type of ironic comedy, a hero leaves a society to start anew rather than stay and assemble the characters of the "old society." Seen in this light, Tom is clearly the hero or protagonist, and his departure reflects a comic narrative strategy. Yet because he looks back on the old society of his sister and mother with some regret and eventually leaves them, the comic dimension of the story is greatly qualified. Looking for larger narrative strategies brings the central conflict back into focus: Tom, the artist-protagonist, wants to establish his independence, while Amanda, the antagonist, wants to secure the family's financial future.

Coincidentally, some of the same narrative elements are to be found in *Nora*. Though she is not an artist, her quest for independence, for personhood, has a romantic quality. Yet leaving the family ends the play with more than a little ambiguity. Once again, we have a hero seeking personal fulfillment, coming into conflict with a parental figure—which describes metaphorically Torvald's relationship to Nora—who demands loyalty to the family unit.

Along with narrative patterns, plays also have archetypal characters. Drawing on an ancient pamphlet called the *Tractatus Coislinianus*, Frye lays out the typical characters of both comedy and tragedy. Since comedy tends to be more formulaic, its characters are usually clear descendants of archetypal groups. These are the *alazons*, or imposters; the *eirons*, or self-deprecators; *bomolochoi*, or buffoons; and the *agroikos*, the churl or rustic. The *alazons* are usually blocking characters, like Egeus in *A Midsummer Night's Dream*, who attempt to impose their will on their children. The hero is often an *eiron*, the opposite of the pompous blocking character and often somewhat neutral compared to more extreme figures. But within the *eiron* group is also the tricky slave or scheming valet, or, like the Duke in *Measure for Measure,* the older man who begins the play by withdrawing from the action and returns at the very end.

Why should these categories matter to the modern director? Because they provide an excellent template against which one can place any character in order to discover its basic type and its individuality. They can also provide clues to the function of each character in the narrative.

MASTERING NARRATIVE

If the director is the author of the play's action, he must also be a master of narrative. If he's industrious, he'll read hundreds of plays, novels, short stories, and news stories and see numerous plays and movies to acquire a deep understanding of the myriad ways that stories are constructed and work on their audiences. Mastering narrative isn't a purely intellectual process; you need to be able to sense the emotional effects that story elements produce. It demands keeping one eye on the story's strategies while also enjoying them. In rehearsals this capacity allows the director to be compelled by the actors' work while simultaneously evaluating it. One of the best ways to absorb a play's story is to memorize the sequence of scenes, the plot, not by rote but by deducing how and why one scene follows another. In this way you learn the relationship between the scenes, their function, and the progression of the narrative.

TIP: NARRATIVE AWARENESS

Giving each scene a name can be an effective aid in learning the story. I would call scene 2 of *The Glass Menagerie* "What are we going to do with our life?" or "Mother and daughter have a heart-to-heart." "The holiday bribe" would remind me of the first scene from *Nora.*

> Other exercises can foster a sensitivity to narrative.
> Adapting a work from another form—such as a novella into
> a play—cutting a classic play (as Bergman did with A *Doll's
> House*), or even writing one's own offer valuable lessons in
> dramatic structure.

ANALYZING A NEW PLAY

The director who takes part in the development process of a new play
bears a great responsibility. Because the script is fluid until it is
"frozen" for performance, the collaboration with a playwright is exploratory yet delicate. I've seen nascent scripts blossom into strong
plays, others never take shape, and many more have their original
spirit surgically removed by development. On the most basic level, a
director needs to make sure the final product belongs to the playwright.

If I've decided to direct a new play, it'll be because I have a
strong affinity for it regardless of where it is in its development. At
first, rather than critique or analyze, I try to learn the play's history—
namely, the impulse that made the author write it. This draws me
closer to the author's original vision and, hopefully, builds trust between us. Only then will I take on the role of the playwright's sounding board, describing why and how the play has worked on me and
might affect an audience. Although it's difficult to predict how the
development process will proceed, it will be smoother and more focused if, early on, playwright and director establish a basic agenda for
the play's evolution. Regardless of how much or how little work a
play may need, writer and director ought to be on the same page
about what must be accomplished.

Perhaps the most difficult question a playwright faces is what to
state and what to imply; in other words, how explicit does the play
need to be? Here the director can aid the writer by reflecting back
what she sees and hears. On the other hand, an insistence on clarity

and conventionality can erase the eccentricities and idiosyncrasies of a play—its individuality. It's important to realize that the director's desire for lucidity may not always improve the play.

Another typical issue with a new work is how well offstage characters and events are handled. Do we know enough about what's happened offstage? Too much? Should an offstage event be dramatized directly? A sensitive director can be a barometer of the balance of exposition and action.

As I begin to analyze a play, I try to articulate the action. This can aid the playwright—who may or may not have been conscious of it while writing—to perceive the through-line of the narrative more clearly. Likewise, I try to understand the structure of the play—how it works. As a director, you can be an extremely valuable resource if you understand how every element of a play functions, how each speech or scene solves a specific narrative problem, and how every part of the play strengthens or weakens the playwright's intentions.

When I directed *The Cryptogram*, I met with David Mamet to discuss the production. Although the play had already been produced, I relished the opportunity to learn about its background and the playwright's intentions. While there were only a few moments about which he made strong recommendations, he insisted that there be no incidental music or sound effects. This puzzled me at first. But as I studied the play, I came to understand his intention: the play's stylized language was the only music he wanted the audience to hear. While a play is going on, Mamet never asks the audience to focus on or think about what is happening offstage in other rooms and other worlds. A key intention, and virtually a convention of his work, is that his language should create its own complete, dangerous, hermetically sealed world.

LANGUAGE

Detailed discussions of language are rarely found in books on acting or directing. For most of the short history of directing, the actor has been deemed responsible for how language is spoken, except perhaps in the case of highly stylized plays. The tendency of many directors to avoid telling an actor exactly how to say a line, so as not to make him seem ignorant or incapable, has also probably contributed to the uneasiness about working on such a detailed level. Yet it's virtually impossible to direct a play of complex language successfully without close textual work. And as a major group of contemporary playwrights migrates away from realism toward greater stylization—Mamet, Shepard, and Churchill, for example—language takes on even greater importance.

Lapses in much of actor training have also made language a pressing directorial concern. Most experienced directors would agree that to produce works by Shakespeare, Shaw, Wilde, and other language-oriented writers, it has become increasingly necessary to rely on a pool of actors who have experience with "language plays" or who have been trained by a handful of the best programs. In response to the naturalistic American writing that emerged in the 1940s and 1950s, much of American acting training has tended to focus on emotion, often excluding the technical principles of language and linguistic style.

A visually saturated culture that encourages sound-byte-sized units of language hasn't made it any easier for the emerging actor. All discourse, including theater, suffers as language, rhetoric, wit, and the written word are devalued. Complexity of thought and expression are now often frowned on as overly learned, and savoring any language other than slang is considered an affectation. As many teachers have noted, the tendency of the modern American speaker is to deaden the poetry and musicality of heightened language by adopting the short rhythms and downward inflections of everyday speech. These circumstances make it imperative that a director have a strong technical grasp of and appreciation for language—and know how to assist the actor in communicating it.

ANALYZING LANGUAGE

Heightened language—the currency of stylized dramatic writing—is characterized by a reliance on imagery and a deliberate attention to rhythm. As an example, one could almost randomly select any line or speech from Shakespeare. Let's consider "What light through yonder window breaks? It is the east, and Juliet is the sun." Here the simplest nature imagery, as a metaphor for Juliet, conveys Romeo's ecstasy at the first sight of his love. The line's emotional energy is reinforced by the way the two clauses in the second sentence balance, indicating his enjoyment of her perfection. Imagery and rhythm work together to express infatuation. To convey Juliet's perfection, an actor playing Romeo would need to emphasize "east" and "sun" and vocally balance the last two clauses. This is a simple example, but breaking the sentence anywhere but after "east" would disrupt the rhythm and diminish the poetry.

With more complicated passages, the actor and director must break the language down into exact meanings (denotative qualities) and their implications (connotative qualities). At the beginning of the process, paraphrasing is often helpful to foster understanding. One of the reasons heightened language is enjoyable to speak and listen to is its complexity of expression. The imagery, like the argument, has a logic—more likely to be emotional than intellectual. Identifying that logic is the work of both actors and directors. As always, analysis must be linked to what is happening in the scene—the action.

Although the industry that has grown up around Shakespearean production has produced a number of rules for speaking the language, few are consistently reliable. One of the most common is that pronouns should never be stressed. It's true that they are not often the key words of a sentence. But when one character has to compare himself to another, the actor has no choice but to stress the pronouns. There are, however, certain *tendencies* in heightened language that you should be aware of. For example, a verb is often the motor of a Shakespearean line. In Claudio's lines below, from *Measure for Measure*, there are three naturally stressed verbs in the first line and two in the second that propel the language forward (the italics are mine):

> Ay, but to *die*, and *go* we *know* not where,
> To *lie* in cold obstruction and to *rot* . . .

TIP: WORKING WITH METER

Meter is a rhythmical structure of poetry that is determined by the number and type of emphases in a single line. In Shakespearean verse, the smallest unit of rhythmic construction is the iambic foot, which contains an unstressed syllable followed by a stressed syllable. The typical Shakespearean line is written in iambic pentameter, meaning there are five iambic feet (out of a total of ten).

These lines from A *Midsummer Night's Dream* scan as follows. (The straight line indicates a stressed syllable.)

> Ĭ ām, m̆y lōrd, ăs w̄ell dĕrīvēd ăs h̄e,
> Ăs w̄ell pŏssessēd; m̆y lōve ĭs mōre thăn hīs

Notice that both lines are "regular," because each contains five iambic feet and the second syllable in each foot is stressed. The continuous flow to these types of lines has a bounce that can enhance a kind of comic patter.

Some lines are deliberately irregular. Among the many possible variations: a line may reverse the iambic pattern, starting with a stressed syllable followed by an unstressed one; or it may contain two consecutive stressed syllables; or it may have fewer than ten feet. These exceptions are never accidental—Shakespeare uses them to signal a change in or heightening of emotion. Ordinarily, we would scan the following line in this way:

> Dŏth w̄ith thĕir dēath b̆urȳ thĕir p̄arents̆' strīfe.

But when we say it aloud, we find that the natural emphasis is different. "Doth" is stressed, as is the first syllable of "bury." "Doth" calls attention to the importance of the line, and the bluntness of "bury" emphasizes the harshness of the conclusion of *Romeo and Juliet*. By varying the rhythm, Shakespeare points up a critical meaning.

Scanning each line is an important exercise for both actors and directors because it's the key to establishing rhythm, which in Shakespeare often contains clues about imagery, emphasis, meaning, and delivery. But meter is not *always* a reliable indicator; the meaning and context of a passage may require emphasizing syllables or words that contradict the conventional rhythm. Scanning lines is most useful as a way of discerning when the lines are regular and when deliberate irregularities signal special occasions and conditions.

Every playwright's language has its idiosyncrasies. Shakespearean dialogue is characterized by—among other qualities—long thoughts, numerous rhetorical devices, rich skeins of imagery, and sophisticated wit. His plays test a great range of an actor's abilities, from understanding rhythmic properties to penetrating convoluted images. George Bernard Shaw's language, though more intellectual than Shakespeare's, is no less passionate and extended. To deliver his long sentences, an actor must maintain energy through to the end. In fact, most elevated language demands continuous vocal energy and upward inflection to the end of a sentence to carry forward complex images and thoughts. The language of David Mamet's plays is highly styled but in a very different way. Its short, terse, aggressive phrasing requires a certain vocal pressure and emphasis—not often found in colloquial speech—to sustain the rhythm and energy. For the director, recognizing the qualities and demands of language is just as important as knowing the type of story a play tells.

To convey the meaning of a line properly—whether prose or poetry—it's critical to decide which words in a line to stress, or *key*. If you disregard or discount keying—as some actors and directors do—an audience will be hard-pressed to make sense of what they are hearing. When actors key improperly, or when emphasis is a matter of interpretation, the director must become involved. The standard rule of keying is that new information should be stressed, but in practice this concept isn't always obvious. Here are some examples from Shaw's *Major Barbara*, about a young, idealistic Salvationist.

After putting up with Barbara's preaching at a Salvation Army yard, a street tough, Bill Walker, warns her fiancé (Cusins) to "stop er jawr; or youll doy afoah your tawm." Cusins responds by teasing Barbara.

> Cusins: I wonder!
> Barbara: Dolly! [indignant in her mother's manner]
> Cusins: Yes, my dear, it's very wearing to be in love with
>   you. If it lasts, I quite think I shall die young.

If you weren't looking for the key word in Cusins's last remark, you might have stressed "think" or "young." But neither dying nor dying young is the "new information" in the sentence. "I quite think I *shall* die young" is the correct emphasis because it is Cusins's consideration of Walker's warning that is new. Stressing "shall" activates the line: it gives the character something to do—namely, consider Bill's advice. It also supports the humor of Cusins appearing to take Bill's warning seriously.

In the same act Snobby Price, a crafty, unemployed painter who frequents the Salvation Army yard for the free food, has convinced an Army officer that he is a changed man.

> Mrs. Baines: Would you break windows now?
> Price: Oh no, maam. The windows of eaven av bin opened
>   to me.

"Windows" and "opened" have been mentioned or implied in the previous line, so the emphasis should be on the two new pieces of information: "The windows of *eaven* av bin opened to *me*." This reading imparts the outlandishness of Price's pandering.

In plays of complex thought, you will need to be aware of *antithesis*, a favorite device of both Shakespeare and Shaw. In her excellent book *The Actor and the Text*, Cicely Berry defines the term as "the contrasting of two ideas by using words of opposite meaning in consecutive clauses." For example, after Barbara's father buys off the Salvation Army with a sizable contribution, Mrs. Baines, the local Army leader, pleads with Barbara not to discard her beliefs: "if you won't come and pray with us, promise me you will pray for us." There is no value in stressing "pray" since it is old information. More to the point, the sense of the line hinges on the antithesis of "with" and "for."

Here's an obvious example from a scene involving another un-employed worker, Peter Shirley.

> Shirley: I wouldn't have your conscience, not for all your in-come.
> Undershaft: I wouldn't have your income, not for all your conscience, Mr. Shirley.

Clearly, to convey the antithesis of ideas, the actors would have to stress "income" and "conscience" in both lines. The conflict in *Major Barbara* is built on antitheses of poverty and wealth, charity and work, marriage and business.

It's an important directorial responsibility to make sure the text is keyed properly. Though notes on keying may seem like minor details, they shouldn't be withheld until run-throughs, because actors cannot play actions forcefully if they are stressing the wrong words.

CHALLENGES

In directing a play, it's easy to miss the forest for the trees. You can get so caught up with the journey of the characters that the play as a whole is shortchanged. That's why looking at it from the outside can provide a fresh point of view. When I adopt an external perspective, I start to notice not only the play's structure but some of its shortfalls or special challenges. Even if all my observations aren't borne out in re-hearsal, my initial evaluation is a starting point for planning the production process, from casting to scheduling. Pinpointing challenges is an excellent first step in setting an agenda and a schedule. If your list does turn out to accurately reflect the major challenges, looking back at it in the midst of the process can keep you on track.

To determine the challenges of a play, I might ask: Is there a weak scene, or an especially difficult one that will require extra attention? Will a particular character need to be highlighted? For an episodic play, have I set aside enough time to work on the transitions? How can the language best be communicated? Does the play present specific technical or logistical problems? A list, whether written or mental, helps foreground issues that, if not considered early on, may cause difficulties later.

Preparation is often the key to avoiding problems and to meeting challenges. During one short scene in the Donald Margulies play *Dinner with Friends*, the characters cook part of a meal. Recognizing this activity as a difficult and important challenge, I set aside added rehearsal time and asked the actors to memorize the scene as soon as possible so they could explore its actions while cutting, chopping, and cooking. As is normally the case, the actors didn't have the actual food until technical rehearsals, but I requested that in the meantime they use potatoes to perform rather than simulate the activity. Identifying potential problems is an organizational skill that is often considered too mundane to teach but that is absolutely essential for every director.

TIP: THE CHALLENGE OF STAGE COMBAT

If a script calls for a physical struggle that entails more than a simple slap, I will bring in a fight director who is trained and certified in the art of creating the illusion of combat in a safe manner. This work needs to be started early in rehearsals but not before the director and actors have had a chance to rehearse the scene to work on the actions. If the fight director has watched these rehearsals, the choreography he invents will be far more effective than if he joins the company "cold." Beware: Staging, coaching, and polishing fights always take more time than you first expect. Actors have varying levels of facility and comfort with stage combat. As with every other aspect of rehearsal, developing trust and chemistry is as important as delineating the moves. It takes time, patience, and an attention to actor concerns and suggestions. Working on the combat at the same time as you are rehearsing the acting tends to create frustration and a loss of focus. Holding separate, regular rehearsals for combat is far more productive. To manage this challenge for a complex altercation in a farce I directed, I set aside a short period of rehearsal nearly every day for two weeks. Like developing a dance routine, creating stage combat requires considerable time and repetition for actors to become familiar and comfortable with every movement.

As you may have already gathered, I believe that one of the chief challenges in directing *The Glass Menagerie* is to get the audience to truly understand and empathize with Amanda. An awareness of this challenge can even inform the casting of the role. Another challenge is deciding how to manage the time differences in Tom's monologues. When he speaks directly to the audience, are we literally in another era? Would he be wearing clothes for that later period that are different from those he wears in the scenes with other characters? Still another challenge is doing justice to the play's poetry, which is more fragile than one initially expects. *The Glass Menagerie* is a memory play, told by a narrator, yet it also adheres to many of the conventions of realism. How do you balance the two? My list of challenges would also contain a reminder to ensure that Laura not come across as a victim.

Every director will have a different list, because a play challenges each director in different ways. Gaining a sense of the potential hurdles will prepare you for design meetings and rehearsals in the same meticulous way that a general might prepare for a battle. In marshaling your army, what are the obstacles posed by the terrain? What are your resources? How well are the troops suited to the task? What must the focus be to achieve victory? In the middle of rehearsals, it can be difficult to see the battle for the skirmishes. Having an initial idea of what problems may lie ahead will help remind you of your goals and priorities.

PART II

PRE-PRODUCTION

FIVE

DEVELOPING THE APPROACH

H aving broken the script down, it is now time to focus on the whole by developing a central interpretive idea, or what I call an *approach*. I prefer this term to the overused *concept*, which, for me, has connotations of a directorial overlay that doesn't always follow from an in-depth understanding.

Because visual images are often the most obvious signs of directorial influence, audiences sometimes mistakenly assume that interpretation exists entirely in the look of a production. When the approach *is* merely a set of visual ideas, it can leave the play unexplored or shoe-horn it into a narrow range of expression. In his provocative book *theatre@risk*, the producer Michael Kustow criticizes an excessive focus on visual aspects:

> The more recent generation of conceptual directors . . . sub-sum[es] everything to some overriding concept which is embodied in scenic design, but under-explored in words. The method works well in opera, where the music articulates what meanings music can, and it makes great photographs in glossy theatre magazines like the large-format German

monthly *Theater Heute*, in which every production looks like
a masterpiece. But unless the spoken text is mimed, it's pictorial drama for a predominantly non- or anti-verbal age.

For many directors, myself included, developing an approach requires multiple readings, research, and the kind of thinking and
imagining that I have detailed in the last two chapters. It isn't unusual for a director to have an intuition about an approach in the
early stages of preparation. When that happens, the action breakdown becomes a way of testing, developing, and adjusting the intuition. An intuition that survives this test may become an approach.
Since it must thread its way throughout a production, an approach
has to measure up to a play's every word and action, illuminating
them in clear and compelling ways.

Because directors often get buried in the details of the design
and rehearsal process, the approach should function as a goal and a
guide through the thicket of moment-to-moment decision-making. It
reminds the creative team of the reasons for doing the play in the first
place and its significance to a contemporary audience. A resonant
approach conveys, whether overtly or subtly, why the play is being
produced at that time.

An approach can vary from an elaborate hypothesis to a detailed
plan. It can be active or recessive. I like to think of it as a framework
for exploration and the basis for working out the production's design.
Some directors claim to start work with blank slates, using long rehearsal periods to discover their approach. This may work for the extraordinarily gifted or those with limitless rehearsal time, but most of
us will want to do some preparation before facing the team of designers we are asked to lead. Thinking about an approach in an unhur-
ried way affords a director the luxury of imagining more than one
possible production—a speculation that will lend substance and re-
inforcement to the choices that are eventually made.

The process of developing an approach is the prelude to working
out a design. And while the director is responsible for all aspects of a
production, she has a distinct choice in developing the visual ele-

ments. She can decide on a concept and hire designers to carry it out. Or she can prepare the play, formulate ideas and possible ways of proceeding, and then collaborate with designers to realize the production's unifying principles. Clearly, my preference is for the second choice, working with designers once I have done some preparation and research.

"There is no collaboration," says the director Mark Lamos, "if you come to the table and say 'I have this idea—and this is how you will assist me in presenting it.' Collaboration is saying, 'I have certain potent feelings about the work, but I don't understand everything.' " Testing out ideas on others is a pleasure and a necessity for directors, especially in conceptualizing and designing, which are by their very nature synthesizing processes. A true dialogue with designers will nearly always lead to a more integrated product as well as a more satisfying collaboration.

Some directors never consider an overall approach, preferring to focus entirely on the microlevel of staging and coaching actors. But without an approach, a director's decisions about everything from character to costumes have little chance of achieving a unified vision. Designers who have worked with these directors have shared with me the frustrations of being told to simply read and replicate the stage directions, as if even that could be done without discussion. An approach is, put succinctly, a point of view. That you need one is evident in the simple fact that every production of a play is different because it is directed by a different person. It only makes sense that those differences should be deliberate.

At the opposite extreme from the no-approach directors are the "conceptualists" or *auteurs*, whose directorial imprint is intended to dominate the play. Between these two ends of the spectrum are the many directors who feel that the difference between an ordinary production and a truly vital one is an exciting interpretive principle, a single, unifying idea. This need not exclude all other ideas. In fact, if a production is to have depth and texture, the central idea must accommodate a range of expression. Making choices necessarily focuses and narrows a play's interpretative possibilities, but it should also provide a rationale for assembling a group of artists to present a particular play at a specific time. You have only to watch an extraordinary production by Peter Brook, Ingmar Bergman, or Trevor Nunn, to name a few, to understand how a powerful approach can completely illuminate a play without overwhelming it.

To create an effective overall vision, an approach must take into account the play's central conflict and have a point of view about its world. As I mentioned earlier, the clash between the protagonist and antagonist that you articulate carries with it the essence of the play's action and ideas. Different approaches can emerge out of the same central conflict, but establishing the central conflict is an excellent starting point for developing an approach. Just by elaborating the central conflict of *Nora* as a struggle between the wife's desire to be a full-fledged mate and the husband's Victorian notion of a patriarchal marriage, we create the seeds of an approach that accounts for much of the play's action *and* its world. That conflict suggests at least one way of designing the set: creating an environment that reflects a typical Victorian male like Torvald with the contrast of a few feminine decorative elements.

Moving from the central conflict to the approach is a step that challenges every director, probably because it is a transition from the rational to the intuitive. I like to begin by thinking about the world of the play as written. For instance, is it one character's world or that of a group or community? Is the environment accommodating or hostile to the protagonist? To me, *Nora* felt like Torvald's world, a space dominated by a man, with some of Nora's touches to relieve the maleness.

SOURCES

Virtually any type of visual stimulation can help open up the world of a play, whether it's referred to in the text or associated with another art form. Sometimes a central image can trigger an approach. For me, the initial stage direction in *The Glass Menagerie* was particularly evocative: "The Wingfield apartment is in the rear of the build-

TIP: READING FOR THE IMAGE

Try reading the play once, at a relatively early stage, for images rather than story and action. Imagine you're shooting a film, and take notes whenever images come to you. Even if the images are never used, you will have begun conceiving the production in physical space. To concentrate on set, lights, costumes, and sound, it's wise to read the play separately for each element. Otherwise, it can be difficult to track the requirements and progression of the design.

ing, one of those vast hive-like conglomerations of cellular living-units that flower as warty growths in overcrowded urban centers of lower middle-class population and are symptomatic of the impulse of this largest and fundamentally enslaved section of American society to avoid fluidity and differentiation and to exist and function as one interfused mass of automatism." When I directed the play, the set designer and I used the beehive image, with its implication of economic deprivation, as an impetus for the physical production because it related to my sense of the central conflict: Tom versus Amanda; the needs of the artist and individual to express himself versus the economic demands of family. The design of the house suggested a confined container surrounded by many others exactly like it. Although the play's socioeconomic dimension isn't always directly dramatized, the characters' economic status underscores the entire play. Certainly Amanda's need to see Laura married and Tom's desire to escape the nine-to-five world reflect their economic plight. Amanda is the center of most productions, but I saw Tom as the protagonist. He is, after all, narrating the story and the only character who exists in the present. He takes us into the past partly out of guilt over leaving Amanda and Laura in such dire financial straits.

As I suggested in Chapter 2, past productions can also fire a director's imagination. I discovered an approach to *The Guardsman* by Ferenc Molnár after seeing photos of the original Broadway design. First performed in Europe in 1911, the play was a precursor to Noël Coward's witty comedies. The central conflict pits a jealous husband, an actor—who disguises himself as a guardsman to try to prove his wife's infidelity—against his wife, an actress, who wants to recapture the adventure and charm lacking in their marriage. Molnár describes them as their country's two most famous actors, yet the set for the American premiere in the 1930s resembled, to my eyes, an elderly aunt's musty, overstuffed attic. These photos immediately made me realize that if a contemporary audience were to accept the ego, jealousy, rivalry, and stature of these two public figures, they would have to be the equivalent of an MGM star couple in a much more glamorous world. I wanted a husband and wife whose every action was an excuse for reaction, who acted out their rivalry in a heightened, theatrical environment.

The style the set designer and I settled on was the glamorous look of art deco, with some modern interpolations. Although we set the production in the second decade of the twentieth century, audiences thought the play had been updated or written much later. In fact, it was architecturally true to the period; in some parts of Europe, the deco style was already the cutting edge. Our own age's delight in art deco lent the production a surprising freshness. The setting reflected the style, elegance, and importance of two celebrities and allowed the conflict of egos to take place in an atmosphere of opulence and drama. I doubt I would have arrived at this approach without having researched the original production. Production history can often be a guide to those elements of a play that are most malleable and that, to a large extent, determine the way various productions of the same play differ. The more malleable features of a play might be its setting, one of its central characters, a key scene or moment, or all of these. Pinpointing them is a way of reminding yourself, while developing an approach, of where you need to make dynamic choices.

METAPHOR

Another way to react intuitively to a text is to invent a central visual metaphor. The beehive image from *The Glass Menagerie* was the author's own, but a metaphor arrived at by the creative team can be just as effective in opening up the world of the play and unifying the design. A recent production of *A View from the Bridge* appeared to use a steel trap as its metaphor. The set, consisting of a series of steel walls and platforms that opened and shut, effectively communicated the protagonist's sense of enclosure in a world of repressed feelings. Peter Brook's seminal production of *A Midsummer Night's Dream* used a stylized gymnasium as its metaphor: with its white box and swing, it emphasized the physical aspects of the play.

With young lovers and a scholar as central characters, Machiavelli's Renaissance comedy *The Mandrake* centers on teaching and learning, and the difference between scholastic and practical lessons. Where better to set a college production of this play about deceit, double-dealing, and betrayal, I thought, than in academia! The design for the production I directed was a combination of the modern and the antique. The hallowed halls of a university were built out of laminated book covers; classical pillars and statues dotted the landscape; and furniture on casters rolled across a carpet of artificial grass. In this case, the metaphor was a place—academia—that, when literalized, became a strong design statement and an effective environment for comedy.

TIME AND PLACE

Making decisions about a play's physical production before deciding what story to tell (with the aid of a central conflict) and before exploring the play's written world can make for ineffective design choices. In thinking about the setting for a production, I ask two questions: How important are the original time and place to the action? And how accessible is the play to a modern audience? If the play is realistic, chances are that the original location and time are critical to the action. By its nature, realism is overdetermined, tied to a complex skein of specific socioeconomic details. Realistic plays usually suffer when directors try to modernize them. The urgency with which Amanda wants to marry off Laura would make little sense in a modern setting. The central actions of that play are very much part of the aftermath of the Depression. With *Nora*, the marital conflict would be less credible were it taken out of the Victorian era.

When working on a play that isn't realistic, however, the accessibility of the original setting becomes a larger issue. The settings for Shakespeare's plays tend to operate as suggestive frames for the action rather than as highly detailed, deterministic environments. He set plays outside England not in order to fully envision Venice, Rome, or Turkey but to use the audience's stereotypical perception about that place as a lens on his own world. When time and place are loosely drawn, the choice of where to set the play becomes crucial and complex.

If the time and place are chosen cavalierly, they will probably be at odds with the action of the play. On the other hand, if the decision is a simple default to the original setting without due consideration, the production is likely to be a museum artifact instead of a vibrant event. This does not mean you should never utilize the time and place as written. In fact, Jonathan Miller, who has updated many a classic, sees more value in *not* transposing a play to a contemporary setting. "By accepting how different the world referred to at the time of writing is from our own," Miller suggests, "similarities, in views and emotional experience, become much more striking." In his revelatory productions of the eighteenth-century playwright Pierre Marivaux, Stephen Wadsworth has brought an inventiveness and exuberance to the original settings that seems almost radical. About locating the plays, he says:

> I just want people to know that you can construct an elegant, visually "traditional" production in period dress and still do *really* aggressive, radical, invasive work. Radical classics doesn't mean only visually extreme; it can be emotionally

extreme, morally extreme, intellectually hot, verbally and rhythmically *wild*.

Even when you choose the original setting, you must still *find* a specific production style. Wadsworth requires himself to "re-envisage, re-imagine, rediscover a style for playing these plays—as adapter, too, not just as director—which honors both where they came from and where they are headed, i.e., into the hearts and minds of an over-complicated, media-drunk, hungry-for-meaning *fin de siècle* culture." The knotty subject of style is tackled more extensively in Chapter 7.

TRANSPLANTING A PLAY TO ANOTHER WORLD

After a play outlives its author and takes on an afterlife, it becomes available to a greater range of interpretation. This doesn't, however, confer upon a director the license to make a classic "relevant" by automatically transposing it to our own world on the assumption that the audience will be unable to relate to the original time and place. This tendency, as Jonathan Miller has noted, overvalues our own time by assuming that a play's concerns are identical to our own. Without deep analysis, transplanting a play to an alternate world can be "too clever by half." Every action and object is given a specific equivalent in its new setting, focusing the audience not on the resonance of the play but on directorial gimmicks. Baz Lurhmann's film *Shakespeare's Romeo and Juliet* is a classic case of this type of interpolation, though it was wittier and more effective visually than many stage productions using a similar strategy. (For example, swords turn into guns with the brand name "Sword.") Changing the milieu sometimes deprives it of ambiguity and the audience of the chance to make associations between the two worlds by themselves.

On the other hand, there have been many successful instances of transposing a play. The New York Shakespeare Festival's production of *Much Ado About Nothing*, directed by A. J. Antoon, set the play in America in the early twentieth century. This gave Benedick's return from war a specificity, delightfully underlining his cockiness.

Depicting the era of Teddy Roosevelt and American muscle-flexing, it provided a context for Beatrice's independent, fiery personality. Other successful Shakespeare productions have used a turn-of-the-twentieth-century style that transmits the sensibility of Edwardian or Victorian times without being tied to a specific date and place. If the setting is loosely sketched in, the audience has a broader canvas on which to project connections between the play and their own world.

TIP: A POSTMODERN APPROACH

There are many ways to invigorate a text without altering the specific time and place. Having experienced postmodernism's mingling of dissimilar styles, audiences seem more capable of embracing a production that contains a variety of modes. Some productions even utilize different styles for individual scenes. A recent production of *Henry IV* and *Henry V* presented the plays as a virtual history of warfare, starting with ancient combat and eventually concluding with the Vietnam War. As long as there is an internal logic and a legitimate rationale, modern audiences can accept a diverse approach to production choices.

A thoughtful director avoids easy ways of making a play relevant yet doesn't shy away from energizing it for contemporary audiences. Just as bad as superficially modernizing a classic is approaching it as a revered object, which produces tentative and bland results. While some traditional theaters and directors still insist on producing plays as museum pieces, relying on the original production's choices, they are, at the beginning of the twenty-first century, increasingly rare. Besides, as Jonathan Miller points out, even if we knew exactly how older plays were produced, today's audiences would see these choices through their own contemporary eyes, not as they were originally intended. Imaginative directors find rich and surprising ways of conversing with the zeitgeist.

CONVENTIONS

Developing an approach and style entails identifying a play's system of artifice—its conventions—often referred to as the grammar of theater. The ruling principle of realism, that what is depicted on a stage represents reality, is itself an artifice. Another convention of realism is the existence of a "fourth wall," an invisible barrier between actor and audience that implies the audience is observing the action without the knowledge of the actors. *The Glass Menagerie* is somewhat more complex than a typical realistic play because Tom occasionally speaks directly to the audience. But within the scenes themselves, the fourth wall remains intact. Shakespeare's plays employ conventions such as asides and soliloquies that also break the fourth wall. A familiar convention of the ancient Greek plays was the chorus, which could function in many ways: as a sounding board, a local community, or a protector of the status quo.

But recognizing conventions doesn't require a director to follow all of them. Bergman's *Nora* is a perfect example. A basic convention of Ibsen's *A Doll's House* is that actors enter and exit the playing space through doors that lead to other rooms in the house. In *Nora* Bergman dispenses with this convention; as mentioned earlier, actors not involved in a scene observe from offstage in full view of the audience. For their own scenes, they simply mount a central platform and are understood to be in the Helmer house. The result creates a style that is very different from that of *A Doll's House*.

Every *production* contains its own system of conventions that includes those assumed by the text and those implied by the acting, staging, and design. Sometimes a director dispenses with a convention of the text at his peril. In a production of *Waiting for Godot*, Didi and Gogo, as played by Robin Williams and Steve Martin, often spoke directly to the audience. While these asides made amusing use of their stand-up comic abilities, they made a hash of the play. Having seven or eight hundred people to talk to made their isolation and resultant despair seem senseless.

Within a single production, conventions must be applied consistently in order for the audience to understand the rules of the story. Occasionally, changing a convention can work as a comic or surreal device if it doesn't seem like a gimmick. Settling on a play's conventions is also a crucial step in elaborating a production style.

TIP: KEY QUESTIONS IN DEVELOPING AN APPROACH

In review, any solid approach should address the following questions:

- What story do you want to tell?
- What is the central conflict?
- What is the present-day significance of the play? Why do you want to direct it?
- What did the action of the play mean in its time?
- What type of play is it? How would you describe its genre?
- When and where should it be set? Why?
- In what type of world should the action take place?
- What are some potential design metaphors from the text—and from your own imagination?

SIX

THE DESIGN PROCESS

One of the joys of directing is working with visual artists, whose contributions give definition, dimension, and variety to a production. Sets, costumes, and lights introduce perspectives and resonances as well as sheer visual pleasure that can be achieved by no other means. Whether at a college, amateur, or professional theater, a director who finalizes an approach on her own will lose much of the benefit of a creative dialogue with invaluable colleagues. So will a director who hasn't become familiar with the script, done some research, and formed intuitive responses before design meetings start. Conversely, designing without adequate directorial preparation can lead to critical mistakes in the ground plan, or to a concept that traps the play.

Directors who have a working knowledge of each area of design, its mechanics, and its possibilities have a great advantage. They are likely to possess an intuitive understanding of spatial relationships and scale, how costumes affect character and gesture, and how light alters an actor's expressiveness. Most designers believe, for good reason, that courses or practical experience in design should be mandatory for directors.

TIMELINE

In the best of all worlds, the approach to a play and its design would develop alongside the rehearsals, so that the actors' insights could inform their work. This can be the case if the rehearsal period is an extended one, as it sometimes is in smaller companies. Unfortunately, the design process is often abbreviated at many theaters. Directors and designers may be selected too close to production deadlines. Geographic distance or previous commitments may dictate that the director begin with the set designer alone. If a production is part of a season, the designs might be scheduled for construction well before rehearsals start. Still, none of these circumstances, even within a limited time period, should prevent a director from retaining the goal of a complete process.

FIRST MEETING

Every set designer works differently, so it's paramount that at your first meeting, in addition to discussing the play, you try to discern a method, come to an agreement on a timetable, and outline a way to proceed. When I directed Tennessee Williams's *Sweet Bird of Youth* at the Williamstown Theatre Festival, the set designer, Hugh Landwehr, and I had less than a month to arrive at a design. Even so, at our first meeting I talked very little about visual ideas so as not to preempt his work. We discussed the central conflict of the play, the major characters, and the play's length. No matter how short the design period, you need to communicate your sense of the action *before* the designer embarks on research and preliminary sketches. Telling the designer the story of the play as you see it is a good way to start. That vision, after all, is what the design must serve. Though we hadn't worked together previously, by the end of our first meeting I felt we both had a clear idea of the story we wanted to tell. Although our schedule was far from ideal, we felt strongly about not eliminating steps in the process.

    Sweet Bird of Youth tells the lurid tale of a drifter and ne'er-do-well, Chance Wayne, who, after living off a faded movie star, Alexandra del Lago, returns to his hometown. There he pursues his former sweetheart, Heavenly, who happens to be the daughter of the town's ruthless political autocrat, Boss Finley. Hugh and I recognized that the central actions of the play were its overheated passions. I stressed that the conflict between Heavenly's tyrannical father and her former boyfriend was a struggle to the death between a stern southern moralism and a desire for fame, adulation, and sexual fulfillment. As with every classic or older play I work on, I wanted to find a contemporary prism through which an audience could gain access to the story. Living in Los Angeles made me think this play, where excess, fame, and celebrity were at war with a firebrand morality, could be startlingly pertinent.

THE RESEARCH PHASE

At the end of the first meeting, Hugh and I decided to scour picture files for visuals that would help us settle on a world for the play. Some designers might have started sketching immediately, but in spite of the looming deadlines, we both knew, as new collaborators, that it was important to allow "dream time" for our imaginations. Our research was to take a number of different directions, but it would be guided by my sense that the actions of the play, set in a small Gulf Coast town, would benefit from a steamy, sensuous, overgrown, and overheated environment.

Hugh's research led him to photos of ramshackle southern mansions where old vines had become part of the structure of the houses; to an old hotel in Nice called the Negresco, fronted by giant palms; to a Moorish residence and a Moorish-style hotel; to once elegant patios now infested with vegetation; and to pictures of wet, moist tropical flora. In the meantime, I was thinking about how to make the sensational action of this darkly comic drama theatrical without veering into camp.

During one reading, I suddenly realized that the plot—a hardened young drifter returns to a town to reclaim his old girlfriend and do battle with her father, the town tyrant—had all the earmarks of a B movie or film noir. One of the essences of noir is that a lurid environment symbolically reflects the psychic pressures on the protagonist. (While the black-and-white noir films of the 1950s usually took place in the *urban* jungle, some later noir films, like *Cape Fear* and *Body Heat*, were set in tropical heat amidst sensuous but threatening vegetation.) In addition to the plot, the expressionistic squawking gulls, roar of waves, and almost omnivorous tropical setting fit the genre.

Modern updates of noir, such as *Pulp Fiction*, have made the B movie a potent narrative for contemporary audiences. Since noir style embraces and even revels in extreme passions and ambitions, I felt it would ground the play's excess and enhance its contemporaneity. The idea of a noir style as the envelope for the action now seemed promising. I shared this thinking with the lighting and costume designers, who supported the direction we were following and provided valuable feedback. With a tropical jungle as our central metaphor, we proceeded to put our approach into practical use in the form of a ground plan.

TIP: THE TRAP OF OVERDESIGNING

There are many ways to overdesign. A set that has too many individualized locations, too many elements, or too much detail can swamp a production. No one design can encompass all the ideas and environmental possibilities that a play suggests. Apart from huge commercial productions intended to highlight spectacle, overdesigning usually occurs when director and designer don't trust the play, or when not enough time has been allotted to work out a unifying idea.

Other productions suffer from "too much of the same flavor." Here a particular design choice—a color, a material, a theme—is so overused that there is no contrast or variety. Without the juxtaposition of some dissimilar elements, designs can become static and overbearing, confusing the story and encumbering the play with a single tone. A recent production of A *Midsummer Night's Dream* used towers of sheer fabric, lit from within, to suggest the forest. While it was an interesting idea, the towers were also present in the court scenes. The result: insufficient contrast between the forest and the court, a crucial design challenge of that particular play.

One of the most evocative sets I can remember was for the Off-Broadway production of Caryl Churchill's *Fen*. The interior scenes were played on real furniture placed on top of furrowed rows of dirt. Even in the interior scenes, the Fen (the lowland farm country in eastern England) was ever present, and the juxtaposition was striking.

Because words and setting together create certain chemical reactions, director and designers must consider how action and language will resonate in different environments and theater configurations. For instance, poetic language is often stillborn in sets that are too realistic. Shakespeare needs room for the language and the ideas to take flight. Comedy demands visual lightness and visual wit. Many a director has had to struggle mightily to release a play's humor amidst a dour set.

THE THEATER SPACE

Our theater for *Sweet Bird of Youth* was the proscenium stage of the Williamstown Theatre Festival, a long, narrow house. My choice, as it normally is with a proscenium, was to set the action as close to the audience as possible, staging most of it in the first twelve to fifteen feet from the front of the stage. This required covering the orchestra pit, which if left open would have created a gulf between audience and performers. Hugh Landwehr had designed many productions on that stage and shared my instinct. Because a proscenium stage is a picture frame, the set would also need to narrow the width to help center the key playing areas.

Whatever the shape of the theater, I try to imagine the perfect space for my interpretation of the play: If I had an open area, how would I configure the audience and the playing areas? Based on the research that Hugh shared, I imagined enveloping the audience in dense tropical growth. But then I wondered whether this would be the best context for the audience to examine the values of Chance and Boss Finley. Environmental staging can integrate the audience and the action in provocative ways, but some plays work more successfully when they are separated. Still, the tropical forest image did get me thinking about how we might capture for the audience a feeling of the characters being enclosed in a dark, menacing environment.

CONSTRUCTING A GROUND PLAN

Usually derived from a visual image, such as a sketch, a ground plan is an exact scale drawing of the set and its relationship to the audience from a bird's-eye view. Most experienced set designers offer a director an initial ground plan, recognizing that the placement of scenic elements is a crucial part of their work. Regardless of your designer's training or inclination, you should be prepared with your own formative plan, or at least have ideas on how the various elements should relate. This way you'll have two ideas to inform the conversation. A good ground plan is usually the result of much tinkering, at the same time that the visual ideas are evolving.

Some directors and designers try to construct a ground plan by replicating the stage directions. This is difficult when the playwright's vision of the locations is minimal, incomplete, or unclear—or, as in the plays of George Bernard Shaw and Eugene O'Neill, so extensive that it determines and limits many acting and directing choices. Further, many plays can be staged in a variety of ways. Stage directions are merely a possible guide to locations. It's up to the director and the designer to select the physical given circumstances that are most useful in communicating the story that the director is trying to tell in the particular style they choose.

A ground plan is rarely easy to construct because it has so many important functions. It articulates the staging's significant physical given circumstances; determines the relationship between the play and the audience; divides the space into multiple acting areas; balances the stage; lends variety to the design; furnishes physical obstacles; focuses the staging; and facilitates traffic flow. It also accommodates and enhances a production's major physical actions, which I call *action imperatives*.

As the designer and I are visualizing the world of the play, I start to work on the ground plan by trying to find ways that the image we are creating can serve the play's action imperatives. Is there a love scene? Does it need a sofa? Is there a physical struggle? How much room will it require? Where will it take place? What is the nature of the entrances and exits? Do they need to be very strong? (Will we need to see a full figure coming toward the audience?) Or can they be downstage, with actors entering in profile? Do we want the cross from an entrance to a particular location to be short or long? Does our interpretation suggest an open space or a confined one? If a play calls for hand props, where will they live? And where can they be hidden if necessary? Providing solutions to these issues will ensure that you have the proper spaces to stage the action. You may find that your ideas about staging create imperatives that are different from those in the script, which is why it's vital to share them with the designer.

A director also needs to take into account the physical impact of certain design elements. The normal rise of a step is nine inches, but when it's more or less, it alters the climb up and down. In a design for one of my productions, I asked for a particular step to be at least twelve inches high so that the actors' climb would enhance the illusion of a parapet. Raked stages change the way actors walk, and when the rake is greater than the standard half-inch-to-a-foot scale, actor movement will be affected dramatically. Directing is often about sweating the details, and the designer should not be the only one perspiring.

In *The Glass Menagerie*, the physical placement of the menagerie is a critical decision. If it's in the middle of the stage, glass pieces may fly everywhere when Tom's coat brushes against it. Laura will spend too much time picking up pieces, and the stage crew will have to retrieve the rest in the dark, making the break between scenes that much longer. Other action imperatives include a long scene between Laura and the Gentleman Caller on the living room floor, significant interaction on the stoop and fire escape, and simultaneous activity in the dining and living rooms. To solve this last, rather tricky problem, a director might divide the stage in half, but doing so runs the risk of losing some of the center-stage playing area and having lengthy scenes take place entirely on one side of the stage. The staging will be artificially confined, and the audience will be forced to look at the same area for far too long. Sectioning a stage into halves works best when scenes are short and the action alternates consistently between the two areas. The usual solution to the dining room–living room challenge is to place the dining room on a platform upstage, so that both areas have strong central playing areas.

Some directors stage an entire play on paper before rehearsals begin, while others feel that such work inhibits the imagination. (With a detailed realistic set, the ground plan itself will determine some of the staging.) During the design process, you must plan, at the very least, how and where key moments (such as the altercation with the menagerie pieces) will be played. Without this preparation, you can paint yourself into a corner, with no way to stage crucial action. And working out ideas in advance won't prevent you from finding more creative solutions in rehearsal.

Given the number and complexity of the locales, *Sweet Bird of Youth* doesn't lend itself to a "unit" set solution: a single environment that stands for all or many of the locations with little or no change. It calls for a hotel bedroom, a terrace off Boss Finley's house, the hotel's cocktail lounge and garden, and a return to the bedroom. Having settled on an overall environment for the play, Hugh and I spent the next few meetings discussing the similarities and differences of the locations and the action that needed to occur in each of them.

TIPS ON GROUND PLAN

- All plays require multiple playing areas. For a realistic play, at least four or five playing areas (defined by "sittables," such as chairs, benches, and sofas) are needed to ensure variety in the staging.
- Keep furniture away from walls so that actors can move around the set pieces, which can then function as physical obstacles and help create tension.
- It's usually problematic to fill the center of the stage with a large object, since it virtually eliminates using the most valuable stage real estate for acting. An exception is when most of a scene can be played on an object such as a bed or at a table.
- To create depth in the staging, place set pieces on at least three horizontal planes: foreground, middle ground, and background.
- Anchor the downstage corners of a proscenium ground plan with a sittable. This encourages the use of the downstage areas and allows a seated listener to cede center stage to a speaker.
- Unless you are emphasizing the squareness of a design, an effective ground plan encourages diagonal lines in staging.

THE DESIGN IN THREE DIMENSIONS

I have often heard directors say, "Was I shocked when I came into the theater and saw the set!" You can avoid unwanted surprises by learning to think and imagine in three dimensions. Practice reading ground plans. Develop an intuitive grasp of the approximate size of basic objects like tables, sofas, and chairs. Know the difference in dimensions between a loveseat and a sofa. Understand how a step with a six-inch rise, as opposed to nine inches, will affect an actor.

One of the best tools for transferring a design to three dimensions is a model. Some designers are reluctant to spend time on models, but most realize their value. Especially helpful at an early stage is a white model—a replica of the theater space with a variety of possible scenic elements, such as walls, platforms, doors, and furniture. A white model affords you and the designer the luxury of trying out, discarding, and selecting the best solutions for the play's action. As the process develops and nears completion, the set designer will usually build a detailed color model. I make sure to spend some time with it before rehearsals begin in order to visualize staging possibilities. A director continues to learn about a play as a production proceeds, which is why she must work closely with designers through sketches, elevations, renderings, and on into rehearsals. In the end, a design will be only as good as the team's attention to detail.

Hugh Landwehr's final scenic design for *Sweet Bird of Youth* was an ingenious series of platforms and walls that created interior and exterior spaces without the need to move much scenery. The container for the design was a tropical grove that served as Boss Finley's estate, the hotel garden, and the terrace outside the hotel room. This design allowed us to create the room by simply wheeling in a bed and dropping in a few set pieces using the theater's fly system. Resembling a color version of the film *D.O.A.*, the set fancifully appropriated the iconography of noir. It featured a giant clock, tilted at an oblique angle, lush but sinister tropical growth, and the ubiquitous window blinds—in this case, twenty feet high—that when lit from behind cast the classic patterned reflection of film noir. The design supported my choice to heighten the lurid, dangerous, and at times melodramatic action rather than play against it.

> ## TIP: KNOWING STAGE MACHINERY
>
> While there has been a trend, partly driven by finances, toward single or unit designs for plays with numerous locations, many plays require multiple sets. For a director to understand the consequences of certain design choices, she must be familiar with the methods of changing scenery. In a multiset design, a plan for moving scenery and executing transitions has to enter into the design process at an early stage, not just because of budget limitations but because the *way* the sets move can be as important an aesthetic consideration as the design itself. When a set is generated without considerable early attention to stage mechanics, the set changes tend to be numerous and long, disrupting the flow and style of the production.

SET CHANGE OPTIONS

There are many ways of changing scenery, from fly systems to hydraulics to stagehands transporting pieces *a vista* (in front of the audience). Before deciding on a method, ask: Is this a play that can sustain sixty-to-ninety-second scene changes between acts or scenes? Does the audience need a break to breathe and absorb? Or as with many contemporary episodic plays, should the play move quickly from scene to scene in order to emphasize its sweep and progression?

My approach to directing *Nora* was to present the play as largely the expression of the female protagonist's consciousness. For this idea to work, the designer and I decided that set pieces needed to float onstage without the help of visible stagehands, as if in a dream. There were many ways to accomplish this; largely for economic reasons, a simple winch drove palettes that held the set pieces. Turntables can be extremely useful because they are — in principle — fluid, quiet, and swift. A combination of flying scenery and large castered platforms, called wagons, is another traditional scene change system. While they can still be useful, they can also be clumsy and slow and evoke the Broadway musical aesthetic of the 1950s.

In directing Moises Kaufman's *Gross Indecency: The Three Trials of Oscar Wilde*, I utilized the actors in changing much of the scenery. It seemed perfectly logical to have the play's four narrators, who help tell the story, bring small pieces on and off. Two lawyers' tables on casters moved quickly and quietly, while two utility tables, set in bookcaselike structures, rolled out like file cabinets.

THE REST OF THE TEAM

Bringing in the lighting and costume designers at an early stage in the design process is not always routine but is extremely helpful. As full participants in the look of a production, they can be a sounding board for initial ideas. Their early inclusion can also save a production untold time and trouble. A simple example: a set designed without the consultation of the lighting designer may not leave sufficient room for the "electrics," the pipes that hold the lighting instruments. Unless the costume designer is involved at an early stage, the set may preclude certain choices of style, color, and line. While the set is usually designed first, lighting and costume designers can and should make important contributions to that process.

Just as the director must discuss with the set designer the story of the play in terms of action, he must also be able to articulate the story to the costume designer in terms of character. (The casting breakdown can be the basis for a more detailed description of the characters.) When thinking about costumes, important questions to ask are: Who are the leading players? What are their relationships? How intimate with the audience should certain characters be? What is their "temperature" relative to each other? How much attention to their wardrobe does each character pay? Are they out of place or at home in their environments? What are the differences between their self-images and how others see them? Which characters are paired, and should they be similar or different? These questions, rather than immediate directorial decrees about color and fabric, are a useful guide to initial discussions. When casting is complete, share your thoughts about the process with the costume designer. Since costume can be a useful corrective to casting, disclosing your reasons for casting and how the cast diverges from your original description of the characters will be of great value to a costume designer. After all, he will be designing for individuals, not for ideal images.

Costume designers are usually faced with early deadlines, but unless the play is a complicated period piece, I always want actors to contribute to the design. When doing a modern play that is mostly shopped rather than built, I like the costume designer to be a "clothing dramaturg," assembling different wardrobe choices for each character and allowing actors, director, and designer to see a variety of options.

Directors sometimes see lighting merely as the illumination of the stage. But light also creates focus, movement, mood, and variety. In order to plan with the designer how lighting will serve a production, a director should know the mechanics of lighting and the kinds of light produced by different instruments and angles. Lighting is the most abstract of the design elements. An exchange of pictorial imagery can be an effective way of talking about it. Again, telling the story of the play and the ways in which it might be communicated should be the basis for early discussions.

To construct a light plot, the designer will need to see a run-through as early in the process as is feasible for the actors. I prefer working with a lighting designer who attends more than one or two run-throughs, observing scene work to see how choices were arrived at. Although many successful designers go from one show to another, taking little time to observe rehearsals, it's possible and advantageous to find those who are open to a fuller interaction.

Perhaps because of the influence of film, theatrical sound design has become an integral part of production. Sound can create mood, underline key moments, and cover scene changes. While some designers are also composers and some composers also create effects, the two tasks are often done by different people. I request a composer for nearly every production because I find that original music creates a unique aural environment. I also relish the opportunity to work with another artist who will observe and respond to rehearsals, then fill in emotional qualities that are only hinted at or even absent in the acting. Music and sound can prove especially effective in fleshing out contemporary minimalist writing.

A number of questions face the director regarding music. Should it be live or recorded? If it's live, is the play sufficiently "presentational" to warrant having the musicians visible to the audience? Should it be period or contemporary? What character(s) should it reflect? Some plays can sustain occasional music underneath dialogue or speeches; many cannot. But with most plays, music can be used as tags or "stings" to highlight the beginnings and ends of scenes and occasionally some key moments. Music can also be overused, as it often is in movies, when it manipulates a single emotional response in the viewer.

Too much of a particular music or sound tends to lull audiences into passivity. For instance, to my ear, excessive pre-show music begins to suggest an elevator ambience and makes it difficult to call the audience to attention and put them in the right mood before the curtain. But when they are used properly, sound and music are potent elements of surprise. I even prefer one musical selection in a production to contrast with all the other audio elements, simply to alter an audience's expectations.

Since all production values contribute to the narrative and all stories have a progression, each design element should also evolve. If a character has several costumes, how will that sequence unfold? What different looks can the lighting produce? In what ways will the set transform? When design elements develop over the course of a production, they help communicate that something has happened, that a significant story has been told.

SEVEN

STYLE

Although production style is one of the most important concepts for a director, textbook definitions are usually fraught with vague generalizations—or, worse, received notions derived from the theatrical past. To complicate matters, *style* is a relative term that, in characterizing a play or a production, is likely to produce significant disagreement. No wonder it's easier to say what style is not than what it is.

Production style comprises the choices a director makes regarding every aspect, from casting to curtain calls. Because visual images are always present, set, costume, and lighting design is often the most assertive ingredient of production style. But for a production to be coherent, the acting style must correlate with the visual elements. An abstract design that houses a naturalistic acting style will send mixed signals to the performers and audience.

The fallacies of received practices of style are most evident in regard to acting. Many college acting programs still teach courses in how to "act style," a vestige of the 1960s and 1970s when educators cast about for ways to train actors who were expected to join newly formed repertory companies. At some schools, style classes focus on

adopting the poses and handling the props of a particular era of theatrical history—Restoration, Shakespeare, Molière, and so on. The
actors stand at awkward attention, raise their voices an octave, and
flail about with handkerchiefs, snuffboxes, and walking sticks. The result is a stultifying external play-acting—featuring clichéd poses and
tableaux—that is unrelated to the specific circumstances of a play or
to the actors' living, breathing, present-tense selves.

In *Subsequent Performances*, Jonathan Miller challenges the received wisdom that the familiar pose of a male actor standing proudly
with one foot forward, hands clasped behind his back, was merely a
picturesque way of showing off his wardrobe. He cites Restoration-era
paintings that suggest many of the subjects adopted the stance while
standing with their back to a fireplace trying to keep their hands
warm! Actors and directors have to be familiar with the manners of
relevant periods when working with a historical setting, but gesture
that is separated from the reality—the truth—of a character's circumstances and desires inevitably produces artificial posturing. Even if
we knew exactly how theater was produced in distant eras, productions that meticulously replicated it would mean little if anything to a
contemporary audience. Style defined in terms of past theatrical conventions is, as Uta Hagen has observed, a *critic's* way of describing
and categorizing a work of literature. For the director, style must be
not a static literary term, but a fluid production tool for communicating the play.

One of the most useful directorial definitions of style has come,
not surprisingly, from an excellent director of classical work, Stephen
Wadsworth:

> Style is often thought to be something different from emo-
> tional truth, but the fact is that style *is* content, there is no
> difference between the two things. A physical gesture, for ex-
> ample, *is* an emotion, must be, and the actor must be able to
> understand how it might even be the very truest, most vivid
> way of accessing the emotion.

In art as in life, style usually denotes a characteristic *way* or manner of doing something. The obvious externals of a production, such as design elements and any consistent manner employed in the acting, will often be perceived as signifying a production's style. But a more expansive and useful concept, articulated by Wadsworth, is that style is how form and content merge, the distinctive way that a production communicates. Or, as has often been said, style is knowing the play you are in.

STYLE IN THE TEXT

Language—vocabulary, imagery, rhythm, and syntax—is a play's primary stylistic element. Understanding the unique ways a playwright employs language is the most useful first step in discovering textual style. Other formal elements, such as dialogue and scene structure, also contribute to the style of a play—as does content. Couldn't we say that the style of Tennessee Williams's middle plays consists, at least in part, of ripe sensuality and highly charged sexual encounters? Surely the focus on the Lie and its cover-up is a large part of David Mamet's style. Might not the style of Noël Coward's plays be defined partly by highly educated and witty characters?

Nor is style confined to plays with elevated or heightened language, though language is the most important stylistic element. Even a naturalistic play contains rules and artifices that constitute its style, although they are mostly masked by the illusion of reality. One of the best ways to identify a play's particular style is to study other plays by the same author. Most playwrights recycle themes, characters, plots, and language. Comparing one play with the rest of an author's œuvre sheds light both on the writer's characteristic patterns and effects and on the idiosyncrasies of that play.

Style is manifested not only in action, idea, and character but also in rhythm, point of view, conventions, and genre. A director often communicates a play's style by framing or emphasizing what she thinks are the important stylistic elements. Some of these elements affect mostly acting, while others impact the design. Language, for instance, is largely an acting issue, though it also affects design because the director and designers are, ideally, devising the appropriate environment for the words. A play's conventions are critical to expressing style. Presented as Tom's reminiscence, *The Glass Menagerie* typifies the memory play, with its poetic language and other conventions such as a scrim and scene titles that create the distance of memory. In modern productions the titles are usually deleted, with most directors regarding them as a youthful, rather obvious experiment in the style of Brecht's epic theater.

As noted in the previous chapter, the style of Bergman's *Nora* is very different from that of *A Doll's House*. The absence of detailed settings; the strange opening image of Nora, like a child, surrounded and sated by Christmas presents; the presence of actors observing the scenes; and the flow of the play, with Nora seeming to will each scene into existence—all these are prominent nonrealistic elements of style.

Very often a play will be written from a single character's perspective. In fact, we can define an expressionist play as the direct dramatization of the psyche of a central character. Even plays that are not expressionistic, such as *The Glass Menagerie*, may still emphasize one character's point of view, which will undoubtedly have an impact on style. Genre is also critical to style. For instance, farce is a subgenre of comedy that employs standard conventions such as slamming doors, physical mishaps, and conveniently timed entrances and exits. To create an effective production, a director must recognize and highlight these conventions.

HISTORICAL STYLES

Theater textbooks often include a section on well-known literary and historical styles. Though theater history is essential for a director to know, it's important to recognize that one can't literally recreate German expressionism, epic theater, constructivism, or Artaudian theater. These terms are more useful in an adjectival way, to help collaborators discuss and formulate a production's style. To some extent, historical styles after Émile Zola were, at least in Western theater, reactions against naturalism and realism.

Representational and *presentational* are helpful terms in articulating style. The former describes plays or elements that attempt an accurate depiction of reality. The latter refers to, for example, direct address to the audience and other devices that call attention to a play's theatricality. Because many plays combine representational and presentational elements, the terms tend to be relative rather than absolute.

TIP: DESCRIBING THE STYLE

In order to collaborate effectively with designers and production staff, you should be able to articulate the essence of your play's production style in a phrase or sentence. When I described my idea for the style of *Nora* as "Nora's daydream/nightmare," the designers had a clear sense of the direction I wanted to take. During technical rehearsals for an adaptation of *The Brothers Karamazov*, I realized we could reinforce the story of the entrapment of the central character by using sharply etched boxes of light. Defining style is a process that begins with preparing an approach and continues until opening. A director will always be clarifying and redefining the style in rehearsals, to influence both the acting and the design elements. This evolution can take place only if the actors are not asked to produce a stylistic end product immediately.

STYLE IN PRODUCTION

When style is translated from words into images and action, it takes on a different significance and effect. A production that attempts to underline each of a play's stylistic elements, will evince little if any emphasis, clarity, or unity. Exploring style is a process of selection, a way of distilling the array of textual possibilities to create a heightened essence embodied in the acting, movement, staging, and design.

Because Shakespeare's plays are simultaneously so dense and so open-ended, they present some of the greatest challenges to forging a production style. This is especially true of the plays he set in ancient Greece and Rome, in which antiquity is portrayed, rather loosely, through the lens of Renaissance England. Many productions of *Troilus and Cressida* work hard to present an authentic Troy, but as Jonathan Miller points out, because Shakespeare's rendering of historical setting is sketchy, "the better the archaeological knowledge on display, the greater the discrepancy between appearance and sound." Miller's own imaginative approach to this play was to combine Renaissance and modern references without actually setting the play in modern times. The Shakespearean era was alluded to in the costume silhouette and details of the Renaissance painter Lucas Cranach, but constructing the uniforms out of khakis evoked the horrors of war in twentieth-century terms.

> The effect was that the cast looked like officers out of *M*A*S*H* in Gothic-style uniform. The Greek encampment was made by using canvas, also indistinguishable from *M*A*S*H*, so that characters sat on upturned ammunition boxes. I even went to the extent of having pin-ups on the wall of Ajax's tent, and showed a large, very rubbed out pin-up photograph of Cranach's *Eve*.

Without literally modernizing the play, Miller's production referred, by implication rather than by obvious statement, to Troy, Elizabethan England, and the twentieth century. An ingenious example of creating a multilayered style.

STYLE IN ACTING

In plays that contain heightened language, the size of the acting is directly related to achieving a successful style. Shakespeare's poetry demands a muscularity of speech that isn't normally necessary for conveying realistic language, while the magnitude and expansiveness of the ideas that the speech expresses require a greater clarity, length of breath, and physical space. If you cast actors in Shakespeare whose experience is entirely in realism, it's likely to have a detrimental effect on the size of the acting and the production style.

On the other hand, size never justifies abandoning the quest for truthful—though not "realistic"—acting, no matter how extreme or unusual the action. Behavior can and must be true to the circumstances of the story, or the play will suffer. Yet a surprising number of directors, when confronted with a highly styled play, whether classic or contemporary, allow actors to don masklike faces, strange voices, and artificial gestures, such as those found in the acting classes described earlier. By *indicating* style rather than embodying it, they generate a surface that ignores any depth and ambiguity that the play may have. This can stem from thinking of style as a set of rules and assumptions from the past or from externalizing certain stylistic elements. Acting in plays of higher style does make greater demands on the performer in terms of language and movement, but it should never exclude the basic principles of action and the quest for truthful behavior.

Nor does acting in plays of high style warrant discarding the process of internalizing action that would be used with any other material. Great acting, no matter what the style, is defined less by clever physicalization than by an inner life and brightness, an incandescence. The director who starts rehearsals by telling his cast they are about to rehearse a style play (and that he already knows the exact style) will probably sacrifice full and truthful acting. One of the primary goals of the rehearsal process should be to *find* a specific style to convey the truth of the play's behavior and circumstances.

In a recent directing book, an author known for concept productions interviewed Robert Lewis, a notable actor, director, and teacher who worked with the Group Theatre in the 1930s but broke off from the Method and advocated a more theatrical technique. The purpose of Lewis's interview, however, was to debunk not only the Method but all acting utilizing inner life. Ironically, Lewis insisted on emotional truth no matter what the style of the play.

> I think it is basic to [have] a sense of truthful communication on the stage. To be able to speak and listen and feel yourself within the truth of a situation. If they are realistic situations, then fine, you're home free. But the theatre is not always limited to that. Therefore, if you have problems with language, abstruse language, poetic language, rhythmic language, movement that is more than just lighting cigarettes and drinking wine but has to do with physical transformation of character, then you have to work to achieve that. I don't mean it must be done *only* physically. You always have to find some kind of inner justification for doing it—which in a way brings us back to our old friend Stanislavsky—because, after all, our behavior does not come just from the outside, but from the inside.

Much of the acting of the 1950s, influenced by the Method, paid little attention to physical expression, fixing mostly on personalization, substitution, and emotional recall. "Style," Stephen Wadsworth states, "had been sidelined, and we were left with some pretty mundane evenings, all earnest searching and not much physical or visual grace, not much musicality, little evidence of the plastic arts, the all-important 'externals.'" The trend in the 1970s toward teaching actors style was very much a reaction to the narrowness of the previous era. But like the Method, teaching acting style calcified until the truths that the externals of stylized plays are meant to communicate often disappeared.

Much American and foreign theater continues to suffer from this hollowness, as some directors—more enamored of promoting a per-

unusual audition.
essential qualities
tanding during re-

ses in casting and re-

by imagining different
mpact they would have.
h a brooding, introverted
macho Tom who is one
e of possibilities for each
ou might cast in a dream
rking with you in under-
acters.

wn is a list of all the char-
l requirements, and their
d community theater pro-
ut the benefit of seeing a
rector to begin to commu-
ed. Since the breakdown is
d an approach, the director
ation. As I noted in the last
point for discussions with

ing breakdown. No matter
iptions succinct while spec-
example here is for the prin-
Barbara by George Bernard

sonal directorial style than expressing a play's truths—impose an external gloss that nullifies the heart and soul of the actor. Instead of embodying characters, actors in these productions engage in what the voice teacher Kristen Linklater has called "outward signage"—the superficial vocalizing of a role without internalizing it. No matter how cleverly physical their work, these actors *exhibit* their characters in a shallow show-and-tell fashion that often calls deliberate attention to an ironic distance between the performer and the role. Convinced that this method is avant-garde—and failing to recognize that the best experimental actors fully embrace a role—these actors and directors seem captive to the surface culture of television, advertising, and computer images. What can mitigate the problem is directorial training that includes a range of acting techniques as well as the kind of process that many actors must use for film, where the camera can instantly expose the absence of inner life. The actors of the Wooster Group, a renowned avant-garde company that produces highly stylized work, have shown that a physical acting technique needn't eliminate inner life. The same was true for the great silent film actors, such as Keaton and Chaplin. Their physical expression, while highly stylized, maintained a connection to inner truthfulness. Thankfully, today's better acting training insists on inner life and truth no matter what the style.

Acting style is most successfully achieved when it emerges directly from playing action, embracing the given circumstances, and respecting language. Style then becomes the distinctive way that a production presents the behavior and environment of a play. The acting and the physical production are treated in a very particular and consistent manner, and key moments, crafted within a selected range of expression, are accentuated with speech and movement that are distilled, deliberate, essential.

For the director, then, style is ultimately discovering and expressing the individuality of each play.

ciate a range an
But as long as en
and are subjec ers
hearsals, the b l.

ter 11, the term it

hearsals.

You can strer on
casting possibilitie te i
What might The G wit
Tom? Or a passion Or a
of the boys? One ang
role is to think of vm y
production. This e wo
standing your prel har

THE CASTINC

Written by the dir akd
acters in a play, ysica
most important fe an
ductions, actors t itho
breakdown, and a e di
nicate a vision of nder
critical to generat n an
should write it du repa
chapter, the brea rting
the costume desig

There are m a cas
what your style, it desc
ifying age, class, a The
cipal characters i Major
Shaw that I direct

EIGHT

CASTING

F ew directorial decisions are as nerve-wracking, subjective, and consequential as casting. The old adage that casting is 80 percent of directing applies only if you select very good actors. If not, it will seem as if you're spending 80 percent of rehearsals compensating for casting problems. In a professional situation, good fortune—namely, the availability of certain actors—helps with casting. But as a director, there are things you can do to increase your chances of finding a competent cast whether you are directing at a college or on Broadway.

PREPARATION

In the professional theater, television, and sometimes film, the time between the hiring of a director and the audition dates may be very brief. Nevertheless, the director simply can't afford to approach auditions cold and expect to see what she needs. Like an actor, she must prepare for auditions by making some suppositions about each character. These suppositions are bound to change, but without them it

MAJOR BARBARA: CASTING BREAKDOWN

Barbara—a fiercely independent, strong-willed, charismatic reformer. Robust, good-humored, energetic, romantic and passionate. A new woman of the twentieth century. Mid- to late twenties.

Stephen—Barbara's brother. A gravely correct young man who has yet to be called upon to shoulder responsibilities or decide his future. Despite his timidity, he takes himself ever so seriously. About twenty-five.

Sarah—not unlike her brother Stephen, she is a conventional person in the shadow of her sister Barbara. Imperious and protective of her Cholly (Charles Lomax). Twenties.

Lady Britomart—their mother. A surprisingly contradictory family matriarch. Well mannered but outspoken; amiable but arbitrary; high-tempered, practical, and worldly, yet naïve about the world outside her upper class. Fifties.

Undershaft—Barbara, Stephen, and Sarah's father and Lady Britomart's husband. A kindly, patient, easygoing, and engaging demeanor masks the confidence, power, drive, determination, and guile of one of the country's captains of industry.

Charles Lomax—a man-about-town with an irrepressible and frivolous sense of humor. A seeming expert with little knowledge of anything. Fiancé of Sarah. Twenties.

> *Adolphus Cusins*—a reveler in the body of a scholar.
> Highly intellectual, high-strung, principled but skepti-
> cal, surprisingly tenacious despite his gaunt physical
> bearing. A man in search of a creed.

NONTRADITIONAL CASTING

Since the 1970s a complex discussion about casting minority actors
has taken place in the theater community. Many directors, myself included, see the need to expand the casting of people of color, not
only to reflect Western culture more authentically but to challenge
an audience's perceptions. Too often in the past, minority actors were
simply not considered for leading parts (other than those calling for
an ethnic character) or even for smaller parts corresponding to roles
they actually fill in society. Most theater artists see a need to overturn
old casting practices, but there is debate about the means. Some
directors practice completely color-blind casting; others wonder if
color-blind casting makes sense in a society whose awareness of race
is still acute. Even minority actors themselves disagree. Most would
prefer casting to be color-blind or, at the very least, consistently open
to minorities. But others feel this undermines ethnic identity, and
prefer working in their own theatrical culture.

In highly theatrical plays, such as Shakespeare's, in which the
ethnicity of characters is rarely dramatized, a growing number of directors see every reason to cast multiracially, even characters within a
single family unit. In realistic work, where the characters' social and
ethnic background is more detailed, this may not always be possible.
Casting requirements become even more specific when a play *highlights* ethnic identity. No reasonable director would cast *A Raisin in
the Sun* with Caucasian actors. But could *Death of a Salesman* be
done with an entire cast of actors of color? The play doesn't emphasize ethnicity, and it is, to a great extent, an American fable. In the

near future, directors will need to be increasingly alert to the ways that social change and resultant audience perceptions create the potential for broadening casting possibilities.

CASTING AND INTERPRETATION

Casting isn't only a matter of finding good actors. Very often an inexperienced director will come up with a unique and elaborate concept and then try to fit a cast into it. For a director's approach to make sense, it must take into account and be influenced by the casting decisions. After deciding that *The Glass Menagerie* is Tom's play, I needed an actor who could carry it off. He had to be able to express loss, regret, sadness, and guilt with a profound depth of feeling. Otherwise, the audience's ability to empathize with Tom would be weakened, and the conflict between Tom and Amanda would be unbalanced.

Sometimes casting must overcome or at least compensate for problematic elements in the writing. A particular actor may be cast to flesh out an underwritten character or to soften the edges of an unrelentingly negative figure. Part of finding the best ingredients for your recipe is having an idea of how they will interact and balance.

When I directed *Gross Indecency: The Three Trials of Oscar Wilde,* I didn't specify physical type in the casting breakdown. Since photographs of Wilde and Lord Alfred Douglas are widely available, I felt that casting actors who physically resembled them would provoke comparisons, turning the play into a historical impersonation rather than a uniquely stylized deconstruction. (This choice also gave me access to a wider range of actors.)

The relationship between the approach and the casting must be fluid. A great actor who comes in with an unexpected and exciting reading may require the director to reevaluate the interpretation of the entire play. An approach is only as good as its ability to unify compelling choices by the actors, and a good director always learns something about her interpretation from the casting process.

CASTING FOR RELATIONSHIPS

Casting can be likened to solving a puzzle: there is a finite pool of pieces from which you must put together the whole. But changing one piece may very well alter the entire picture, so it's important to make most of your casting decisions within a short span of time. If you can't secure a key member of a relationship, you'll probably need to put off casting a complementary character. Casting with relationships in mind is critical to a family drama, but it pertains to every play that has more than one character. A director needs time, especially in the later stages (callbacks), to compare and contrast, mix and match. You certainly would not want to cast the three sisters in Chekhov's play without trying out various combinations of actresses in the same room and at the same time.

SKILL AND TYPE

One director's conception of a character's type may be considerably different from another's. This means that directors have leeway when it comes to finding the right actor. For Harold Clurman, type was a matter of inner disposition as much as physical attributes. He advised trying to discern an actor's metabolism, his drive, habits, instincts, and tendencies. You may find a way to tell your story with an actor who doesn't represent what most people see as the appropriate type — and in so doing trigger a fresh and exciting approach to a familiar play. Many of Shakespeare's characters, like Hamlet, are so rich and expansive, the options are almost endless. But always the choice of actor affects the approach to the play. Is Iago, Clurman asks, a fiend, a playboy, or a colorlessly blunt military man? Is Lear a "decrepit old fool, a heroic patriarch, a nice old papa cursed with nasty kids or a monster of pristine pride"? Most Iagos and Lears will be some combination of these types.

Casting for type or for the best actor is rarely a clear choice, but no matter how close to your ideal image an actor comes, it will matter little if she doesn't possess the requisite skills and range. The mistake of casting an unskilled actor ramifies in rehearsal, when that actor's shortcomings can retard the work of the other actors. Another common mistake is casting an actor solely because a single aspect matched the director's original conception. Unless the actor is capable of making adjustments and playing other colors as well, there is a risk of one-dimensional work. It is generally wiser to cast the supple actor than the accurate one. I look for skilled and well-trained actors, partly because most of the plays I direct contain complex language.

Since comedy requires a specific set of acting skills—the most important of which is the ability to play truthfully while releasing a play's humor—it's particularly complicated to cast. Some actors have a knack for comedy, while others do not. Rarely is rehearsal time long enough to teach comic technique, and having to explain the humor of a play to actors will make for a very long process. When an auditioning actor plays down the demands of comedy, insisting that mere truthfulness will suffice, it may signal a lack of skill or confidence. In casting a comedy, in addition to basic skills, I look for an innate sense of humor and a joy in playing the genre.

CASTING IN THE PROFESSIONAL THEATER

Nowadays most professional theaters employ a casting director. This person sets up auditions, recommends actors, and hopefully works with the actors' agents to promote the show to their clients. Some casting directors bring to the job a fount of knowledge of actors and a willingness to search for others when needed. Others schedule the same actors for virtually every project they work on and do not see enough theater and film to broaden their pool. Regardless of whether a theater hires a casting director, it is the director who is ultimately responsible for casting. She must take the lead in ensuring that the talent pool is as large as possible, submitting her own list of actors that includes both ideal and realistic possibilities for each role. Young directors at all levels are usually surprised at the degree to which casting tests their resourcefulness. No matter what level of production, good casting requires attending many plays, keeping files of programs and résumés, and consulting every possible source for ideas.

In university and community theater, an audition often starts with an actor performing a monologue. Then, as in the profession, it proceeds to a reading of the play that features specific characters ("sides"), followed by a series of callback readings for the strongest contenders. The choice of sides should be made by the director, since he must decide which aspects of a character he needs to see in auditions.

TIP: CHOOSING MATERIALS FOR SIDES

There are several schools of thought regarding the selection of material to be read for auditions. Most directors choose a scene from early in the play for the initial reading and a later or climactic scene for the callback. My inclination for the callback is to select a scene that is emotionally charged. If an actor cannot internalize the material, you're much better off knowing it in auditions. When the role includes monologues, you'd do well to have the actors prepare one of them — as well as the callback scene. In casting one modern play with a two-page monologue, I found a surprising number of actors who seemed uncomfortable with the volume of words. By including a monologue for the callbacks, I was able to discover which actors really enjoyed using language.

THE AUDITION

The professional casting process can take a couple of days, a couple of weeks, or even months. The initial readings are an opportunity to begin the culling process and hear how the play sounds. As enervating as auditions can sometimes be, I would rather see more actors than fewer. Directors and casting directors too often peg actors for certain types of roles. You should have enough initial audition time to see a range of actors, including some who might not seem exactly right for a particular part.

In an audition, the actor is escorted into a room, about fifteen feet by twenty, and is introduced to the director, casting director, and producer or artistic director. If a scene has more than one character, another actor, hired by the casting director, will be seated close to the casting table, to read the rest of the lines, so the auditioning actor can be featured. I like to greet each actor, make sure they have the correct side, and offer them the choice of standing or using a chair. To respect any preparation the actor may have done, I try to limit socializing until after the scene is read. I also prefer to answer only simple or technical questions before a first reading so I can see the actor's initial take on a role. If the actor reads the first scene proficiently, I may ask for a second prepared side (other than the one saved for callbacks), or for the first to be read again with an adjustment: a different tack, usually a change in a given circumstance.

The audition atmosphere should be cordial without being overly casual. Important business is being transacted, but there's no reason to be chilly or intimidating. Auditions should not resemble those of lore at which a frightened actor entered a huge theater, looked into the dark, and waited for the director, who was usually slumped in his seat at the back of the house, to ask what he had prepared for the oc-

TIP: READING A RÉSUMÉ

An actor's résumé contains all sorts of useful information, including a list of roles played, level of experience, and training. It's probably most useful as a rough guide to the types of work the actor has done. Some actors list directors they've worked with, and you shouldn't hesitate to contact others who've worked with an actor for reassurance or more information.

casion. Because it is important to work with dedicated actors, I also try to determine an actor's interest and attitude toward the play and the roles, as well as any doubts they may have about working on the project.

Immediately following the audition, it may not be possible to decide whom to call back, especially if the bar has not yet been raised. But by keeping notes on each actor, including vocal and physical attributes, you should be able to construct a callback list by the end of the day. You can always add to the list after the initial days of auditions are over, but by the time callbacks begin, you should have at least several actors reading for each role. Otherwise, you may need to reopen the casting search.

Callbacks permit the director to take a second look at the actors and to have a chance to work with them. You'll need to schedule more time with each actor—or at least the most serious contenders— than in the initial audition. This will allow you to probe different sides of an actor's work and see how he takes direction. Giving an actor "homework" after the first audition can make it easier to see another facet of her work. The casting director will probably be willing to call the actor or her agent and pass on the assignment. This practice is just as useful in university and amateur theater, though there may not be a casting director.

Let us say Actor A auditions well for the role of Tom in *The Glass Menagerie*, but you're not sure he can manage the character's vulnerable side. You could simply ask to see more vulnerability, but a more specific strategy would be to give the actor an adjustment for the callback scene that would elicit vulnerability. For example, at the top of scene 3 you might ask an actor to work with a strong internal obstacle, such as an empathy with Amanda's failure to sell a magazine subscription. Or you might choose a new scene that elicits vulnerability. Young directors sometimes make casting decisions without uncovering enough facets of the actors. The more information you have, the sounder your casting choices will be.

Auditions are for the benefit of the director. Do not lock yourself into a rigid plan when you can learn more by changing it. A strong actor who auditions for a role for which he isn't entirely suited could be considered for another part. The actor will then need additional time to prepare—ideally, several hours or overnight. "Cold" (unprepared) readings—a typical practice in amateur and academic theater—are of little use to the actor or director.

On some occasions, more than one set of callbacks becomes necessary. There may be a wealth of good candidates, all of whom deserve another look. Or perhaps an important aspect of a character hasn't yet been unearthed. Or maybe the appearance of a certain actor at an audition simply did not jibe with your image of the character: his clothes were wrong, or he didn't shave that day. It may seem strange, but these kinds of discrepancies do fool directors and producers. I can think of numerous times in which a producer was surprised at the strength of an actor's callback after having largely discounted the initial audition because of the actor's appearance. I must confess to a couple of instances when I asked actors to return to read again with an altered appearance, because I wasn't completely convinced of their physical appropriateness for a role. While it's best not to waste anyone's time or raise false hopes, you must feel secure about your casting choices. As in all aspects of directing, mistakes are inevitable, but you can minimize them by investigating an actor thoroughly and then trusting your instincts.

SUCCESS AND FAILURE IN CASTING

For many reasons, success or failure in casting may occur with virtually the same pool of actors. One director may be capable of imagining an actor's potential, while another is too literal-minded to cast the better actor over the right physical type. Or, ideally, a director brings to casting a formative approach to the play that includes a grasp of the function of each character within the story she wants to tell; while another, without any interpretive foundation, makes ad hoc and arbitrary decisions. Some directors make better use of auditions than others. It takes diligence and work to size up actors beyond a superficial understanding. Many directors sit back and demand to see a performance, instead of deciding what they must know about each actor and how to obtain it. Offering an actor an adjustment, even one that isn't entirely relevant to the scene, will likely elicit new and possibly valuable information.

Probably the most decisive factor in ensuring successful casting, whether in professional or in amateur theater, is a familiarity with the acting pool. Nothing, not even auditions, substitutes for seeing an actor's work in production. Part of a casting director's job is to be aware of the body of work of the actors who audition. But finally it is every director's responsibility to keep abreast of various pools of actors. With the decentralization of American theater has come an emigration of talent from New York City. For a recent production I directed, we held auditions in New York and Boston, yet we cast four out of the five major roles by videotape and made offers to actors from other cities. The lead in another production was scouted by the costume designer, who had heard about him from friends in a shop in Seattle. As actors scatter across the country, casting abounds with these types of stories. Building relationships and maintaining contact with actors, reading reviews, and keeping one's ear to the ground are essential for successful casting.

PART III

REHEARSAL

NINE

THE EARLY REHEARSALS

F ew people would disagree that the single most important role a director plays is to lead rehearsals. Yet many directors have surprisingly little knowledge of the various ways actors work and of the most constructive ways to communicate with them. Just as shocking is how many highly reputed graduate training programs fail to teach such basic principles. Technical, result-oriented direction—urging actors to be louder, faster, bigger, or more intense—is occasionally necessary and acceptable, particularly later in the process, after actors have been grounded in the actions and circumstances and the emphasis is on sharpening performances. But a steady diet of this type of direction invariably produces generalized, overwrought acting. For the most part, a director obtains superior results when she translates an awareness of the emotional currents of a text into playable actions. No matter where they've trained, most experienced American actors understand and work with action as a fundamental tool, whether the play is by Shakespeare, Molière, Ibsen, or Mamet. And a director who solicits actions rather than results gives actors a greater opportunity to make their own contributions.

Breaking down a scene in terms of actions, as presented in Chapter 3, is a preparation for rehearsals rather than a prescription for directing actors. As actors begin to play a scene, stringing together moments in ways you hadn't imagined, it takes on an entirely different dimension. What happens in front of you in the rehearsal hall—not your preparation—should be the basis for working with actors.

This chapter covers the initial phase of the rehearsal process, illustrating a technique for directing actors using three basic tools: action, obstacle, and given circumstance. The particular sequence is bound to be different for every director; there are probably many ways to use these very same tools. Though I outline a progression for the sake of discussion, even my own practice—and yours—will undoubtedly vary depending on the material, the cast, and the schedule.

DAY ONE

I consider my role at the first rehearsal to be that of a host, bringing together actors who may or may not know one another and encouraging their interaction. Most of them will be nervous, no matter how experienced. Those who have worked in a theater with a resident company of actors who are familiar with one another know how much more anxiety-producing it is for actors and director to begin as strangers.

In many theaters the day begins with a traditional "meet and greet," in which the cast and the theater's administrative staff assemble. In professional theaters there is an additional meeting requiring members of Actors Equity to elect one of themselves as a representative or "deputy." It's usually best to get this and other administrative business out of the way before work on the play begins.

An important task, but one that is sometimes neglected, is reviewing the schedule with the cast. Certainly if you were taking a trip you'd want to be familiar with the itinerary. Actors need to know the various segments of a rehearsal schedule, when run-throughs will begin, and the deadline for being off book. (A small minority of directors require actors to learn their lines before rehearsals. This has always seemed counterproductive to me, because actors who have difficulty learning lines in a neutral manner may be saddled with permanent line readings. Lines learned in conjunction with action should eventually seem inevitable.)

At the first rehearsal, or soon afterward, the set design is introduced to the cast, using a model or a ground plan and renderings. The costume designer also presents a vision of the characters and their world, although a truly collaborative designer will want to observe the actors in rehearsal before settling on final images. For large period shows, costume building may have to begin before the actors arrive. Even then, I try to keep some options open until the actors have had the chance to offer their thoughts. Springing very specific ideas about wardrobe on actors who may not yet have given much thought to character can produce concern and confusion.

The conundrum of the first rehearsal is how much talking and how much reading to do. While some directors discuss the play and their approach before the read-through, I simply offer my reasons for directing the play and convey my excitement about the cast and project. A read-through at the first rehearsal is a matter of tradition or preference, not necessity, unless the playwright is present and can benefit from hearing the play read straight through. When the absence of one actor dictates starting with individual scene work instead, I've found that the cast doesn't necessarily miss having a read-through. Often one or two actors at a first read-through will have a definite take on their roles, which can prove embarrassing to those who do not. While I generally prefer to schedule a read-through on the first day, I try to defuse some of the tension by requesting that the actors not perform but simply read the play for their own sense and understanding and share it with their scene partners. It's a good idea to seat actors who are in the same scene near each other so they can interact easily.

Cutting dialogue from a period play is most easily accomplished by sending your version to the actors before the first rehearsal. It can be harder for actors to cut lines once they've learned them, and reading your version beforehand gives the actors time to understand the reasoning behind the changes. In addition, actors will need to be notified in advance if an accent is to be used. (Plays set in Britain or Ireland are virtually impossible to do without the appropriate dialect—and a dialect coach.) The first read-through is an opportunity for the dialect coach to listen to the cast and take note of the sounds the actors will need to work on. It's also a good time to deal with difficult pronunciations and questions about particular references.

The first read-through can be beneficial to an alert director. (Of course, it can also be excruciating, if an actor is far off course.) Here both the energy of the play and its challenges begin to emerge. The reading can also suggest how rehearsals might proceed and which scenes will need the most work. Some directors gaze at their script during a read-through, but there's far more to be gleaned from observing the actors than following the text.

After the reading, I compliment and congratulate the cast. If the playwright is present, she may wish to offer some encouragement. Then I share some thoughts on the play, trying not to limit the actors. I keep my commentary short and general for several reasons: the actors have other things on their minds; they're better off coming to the play with open minds than with a theory; and a detailed discussion will be premature. My remarks will hopefully begin to move us toward an agreement on fundamental assumptions about the world of the play.

Sometime before rehearsals begin, I'll ask a dramaturg to assemble a stimulating collage of photographs and paintings. At the first read-through, I may distribute background information and urge the actors to continue to work with the dramaturg if they feel the need for further research. Occasionally, directors engage actors in improvisations based on the play's background. Given the tension of the first day and the pressure on actors to absorb a new play, new colleagues, and a new director, I limit the work to reading and discussion.

As the activator of the text, a director must share with actors his enthusiasm, energy, and willingness to grapple with the unknown; the director who doesn't is essentially a contradiction in terms. Too often directors settle for what they think their actors can accomplish easily, though art is rarely produced that way. It's natural and wise to lead actors from their strengths, but encouraging them to work toward comfort rather than truth, depth, and ambiguity usually produces mediocre results.

Directors can make two mistakes in early rehearsals. Some directors want to make friends with the actors so badly, they devote the first day to socializing. (I know a few directors who continue this practice into the second week, forcing the actors to take control of rehearsals.) Others deliver long-winded lectures to impress the troops, turning the rehearsal into a classroom exercise. The challenge of the first meeting with a cast is to balance enjoyment and excitement with an unassuming sense of leadership. To be successful, a director must find a way to lead without being either boorish or frightened.

The first week of rehearsal can be challenging for any director. Those actors who haven't worked with you before may be wondering if you know what you're doing. After all, they've probably worked with directors who don't. You may suddenly be unsure about casting an actor whose new tack on the role bears little relation to his audition. Or after hearing the reading, you decide your initial ideas about the play are groundless. If you direct long enough, all these predicaments are bound to happen. You needn't worry that they spell the end of a career.

TABLE WORK

At the second rehearsal, I continue with table work: reading and discussion. With a Shakespeare play, this stage continues for some days until the cast becomes comfortable with the language. It makes little sense for actors to move around when they aren't sure what they're saying. The less experienced the actors are, the more time you will need at the table. When working with professional actors and a relatively accessible script, I stay at the table for only as long as it takes to move through all the scenes with brief discussions. (Some directors work at the table for weeks until actors are desperate to get on their feet. I find this even more incongruous than blocking the play on the second day of rehearsal because physicalization is essential to playing actions.) The smart director will always play it by ear, sensing when the actors are able and eager to move to the next stage.

Your contributions at the table may well be modest. At this stage you are still soaking up the actors' impulses, and the cast can absorb just so much without being on their feet. In addition to assuring basic sense and comprehension, you may want to discuss the most important beats or the events of the scenes or their functions. You could also ask probing questions to promote what Uta Hagen has called "particularization." This involves making all aspects of a role specific and personal, and it provides the initial context for understanding the action—the muscle for the spine. Even if you believe strongly in a particular action, an actor may have trouble understanding or playing it without sufficient context. Failing to allow or encourage an actor to engage fully in this process early on can backfire in later rehearsals, when she suddenly becomes unsure of action or motivation. It's important, however, to recognize that this work can only *start* at the table. Developing it will take time, trial and error, and physicalizing.

In fleshing out the particulars of character, some actors and directors get caught up in details that have no bearing on the play. What a character eats for lunch or what car he drives isn't worth thinking about, unless there's a scene at lunch or about his driving skills. You'll maintain focus and use your time more efficiently by investigating those circumstances that directly reveal the motives for and ways of playing the actions.

In the second scene of *The Glass Menagerie*, Amanda was to attend a meeting of the Daughters of the American Revolution but became too distraught when she stopped at the business school. To fully appreciate her values and the significance of missing a meeting, an actress would need to address, either on her own or with the director, such questions as: What is Amanda's position in the DAR? How long has she belonged? How important is it to her? Since we hear little more about her social activities, we may assume it's critical to her self-image. An actress who doesn't relate directly to the DAR might employ a strategy popularized by Stanislavski: suggesting an "as if," a more accessible equivalent—in this case, perhaps, a modern women's organization. The process of personalizing will take longer than a single discussion and will play itself out over the entire course of rehearsals. But focusing on the critical references can produce probing questions that stimulate rehearsals.

For the actress playing Laura, a crucial given in this scene is Rubicam's Business College. She spends only one day there, fails a typing test, and becomes sick. An actress must be able to imagine Laura's fear of the college or she will find it difficult to play the scene, with its account of that day and the need to escape. Other references in scene 2 that need to be explored include—for Amanda—the typing teacher, for Laura, the park, the zoo, and the movies.

Some directors believe this kind of work is entirely the actor's domain, that the actor is exclusively responsible for the role, and that the director's job is to stage and pace the production. Certainly, extraordinary actors might be able to make specific and credible all the given circumstances and everything they come in contact with. (A talented actress once told me she had a relationship with every prop and furniture piece on the set.) And if you are fortunate enough to work mostly with a single company, the actors—knowing your expectations—will probably take on greater responsibility. But in most cases, some references and given circumstances will need investigating. Without engaging in an actor's moment-to-moment choices, it's difficult for a director to land the larger interpretive decisions and tell the story decided upon. A perpetual myth is that the best directors sit back, relax, and let the actors do all the work, occasionally lobbing in a brilliant insight. The director who takes this route will likely be rudely awakened by the realization that not even the best actors can direct a production, and that directors and actors cannot communicate by telepathy.

This doesn't mean the director should insinuate himself into an actor's personal life, or do the actor's work for or alongside him. A sports coach is an apt metaphor for a director. A coach observes and shares his perceptions with an athlete. He suggests adjustments to improve the performance. And, perhaps most important, he encourages and inspires, keeps the athlete honest, and urges her to stay the course. Ultimately, it's the athlete who plays the sport. As director, my primary role in early rehearsals is to ask questions and energize actors by articulating the actions and circumstances in vivid and concrete terms.

TIP: PROPS AND FURNITURE

Once the reading tables are cleared, the actors will immediately need a sense of the stage space, set pieces, and furniture. By that time, the stage managers should have taped the floor to indicate the set and procured rehearsal props. (The actress playing Amanda will need to use a coat early on to help her with the reality and timing of coming home.) Real objects make it possible for the actor to *do* the activities and play the actions, not approximate them, and to construct behavior that will ground a performance.

GETTING THE PLAY ON ITS FEET

Getting up from the table is often a slightly discomforting experience. Actors don't always feel ready to move around, and the director may wonder if enough time has been spent in reading and discussion. To alleviate some of the uneasiness, I keep a table off to the side just in case I want actors to sit back down and read a scene again or start by reading through it and then getting up on their feet.

Whenever you enter an unfamiliar space, even with a clear objective or agenda, you need to become familiar with the surroundings before embarking on an important task. So it is with actors who have just left the table and are about to explore the context of a scene. I find that an effective way to start with actors on their feet is to suggest actions that help explore a key given circumstance, such as the location or the immediate previous action. Actors can't *play* given circumstances, they can only play actions. But choosing and playing effective actions doesn't always come easily. If, however, your actors are absorbing key circumstances right away, you can move forward until the actions become vague or uncertain. Whenever that happens, the astute director will formulate new actions that bring into play the context—the circumstances—of the scene.

As I noted in Chapter 3, the given circumstances include everything of consequence to a character at the beginning of and prior to the scene. They include relationships, previous actions, and the environment. Even weather can be important: heat, cold, and the seasons affect characters. You cannot explore all the given circumstances at once. Though every scene has a locus of givens, one or two are bound to be more significant and immediate than others. It's these I try to focus on at the beginning.

The early stages of rehearsals are like sketching—you get raw material onto the canvas to examine and shape. There are no rules for organizing this work. The first few times you run through a beat or a scene, you could test different actions while concentrating on a particularly important given (such as the Rubicam's Business College incident), and as actions are played, a loose beat structure should emerge. During this period, I continue to ask myself, *What's really happening in this scene?* as a way of getting the actors to think about the action embedded in the dialogue. In the first week, I try to build an overall framework of action for much of the play rather than let a small section stall rehearsals. Stopping actors to craft a moment or line when they first get on their feet can make the process very tedious.

In starting work on the second scene of *The Glass Menagerie*, I'd want to see how the actress playing Amanda emotionally incorporates the visit to the college. Should she have difficulty, I might ask: How long ago did the visit take place? Was it three or four hours ago or a matter of minutes? How did she get home from the college? Did she walk? Did she take a streetcar? In order to keep the given circumstance potent, we might decide that the visit took place just half an hour before and that she walked home steaming. So when she enters the apartment, she really needs *to wake Laura up, get her attention,* or *eliminate the pretense.* (If the visit took place many hours before she returned home, she could have cooled off, making it more difficult to justify the actions.)

Notice how important it is to work on actions in conjunction with the circumstance that directly precedes the scene—and how, in turn, considering the givens provides a path to discovering the action. As rehearsals progress, you may find other significant circumstances and different actions. But by focusing on the important references, you've made a start on investigating the scene.

If, as it seems, Laura is surprised by Amanda's entrance, what was she doing prior to it? The stage directions indicate that she polishes her glass collection and plays a record on the Victrola. If it's a favorite, her mood may be upbeat and thus, conveniently, in direct contrast to Amanda's. Is it necessary to delve into these activities? It is if the actress doesn't sense what engages Laura, what makes her happy, and what constitutes the very hermetic world she lives in.

Laura's activities must produce some joy, or she will seem pathetic and there'll be little contrast between her and her mother at the beginning of the scene. If she lives in terror of being caught by Amanda, the contrast between the opening moment and the rest of the scene will also be lost. Why is contrast so important? Because it lends variety and depth to storytelling. It's surely one of the cardinal laws of directing.

As you can see, the text provides some of the basic circumstances, but it's up to the actors and the director to choose which to emphasize, to make them specific, and to add others to fill out the lives of the characters. In scene 3 of *The Glass Menagerie,* Amanda accuses Tom of sabotaging their future with his poor work habits at the shoe factory. Furious at her invasion of his life, he flees. After a monologue by Tom, the scene begins with Amanda trying and failing to sell a magazine subscription on the phone, an event that certainly colors her subsequent behavior. Another telling circumstance is that, the day before, Amanda confiscated Tom's books, believing they were the source of his "depravity."

Thus the scene starts with great force and conflict. Terrified that Tom may be drinking—his father's affliction—she accuses him of spending his nights doing something other than going to the movies. Tom is furious because nothing is off-limits to Amanda. If after some work the actors don't realize the important consequences of this showdown, you may have to explore what it means to Tom to have his books confiscated. Is it the first time it's happened, the most flagrant invasion, or the final straw? And what did it mean for Amanda to discover the books? Did it confirm a suspicion that he'd been lying to her all along? Once the actors truly embrace the given circumstances, the *stakes* become more apparent. (More about stakes in Chapter 11.)

TIP: ONE THING AT A TIME

An effective way to rehearse, especially early in the process, is to concentrate on one element—for instance, one of the immediate given circumstances—at a time. Otherwise the playing may not reveal which circumstance is most important. And remember, your actors are trying to absorb a great many things in a still incomplete context. Later, when they have a more advanced sense of each scene, you can layer in the more subtle circumstances, actions, and aspects of the relationships.

Encourage the playing of one clear action rather than a series of contradictory desires. A direction such as "Excite her, but keep your distance, and also find out if she's available" is far too complicated and qualified to play.

REINFORCING THE ACTION

In scene 3, after the monologue by Tom and Amanda's phone call, the first beat begins with Laura warning her mother that Tom is trying to write. Nevertheless, Amanda walks over to adjust Tom's lamp anyway. The beat seems to end when Tom says "What in hell!" Before that, we might describe his action as *pleading with his mother to leave him alone.* (He actually uses the word "please" twice.) But with "What in hell . . . am I supposed to do?" he *demands that she stop pestering him.* Is Amanda trying to be a nuisance? Hardly. How do we know? That action is unlikely to fit within any superobjective for her that we could reasonably imagine. If her goal is *to hold the family together* or *to secure the family's future,* you can see that *making a nuisance of herself* wouldn't aid those objectives. Yet it's surprising how many times I've seen an Amanda nagging Tom in an almost malicious way. This is probably because the director or actor has an image of Amanda as an overbearing, insensitive mother. But analyzing the scene in terms of action rather than character doesn't bear this out. Concerned about Tom's health, Amanda probably moves the lamp closer to him and attempts to straighten his posture to *make him pay attention to his health.* Nor can the actor playing Tom lash out at Amanda in this first beat. If he does, he'll have nowhere to go when the conflict really heats up. Playing the first beat confrontationally illustrates the mistake of going for the result (the conflict) rather than playing appropriate actions for each beat and letting the beats of the scene progressively build the conflict.

A change of action by one character always necessitates a change in the other character's action. (Laura is present in this scene, but she is merely a bystander.) Once the beat changes with Tom's "What in hell," Amanda's action changes as well. She *confronts Tom with his contemptuous behavior* or tries to *knock some sense into him.* She then discloses that she returned a D. H. Lawrence book to the library. Is this a new beat because there's a subject change? No, because her *action*—*confronting* or *knocking sense into Tom*—hasn't changed. (A single beat may contain multiple subjects.) Why does it matter? Because actions are usually clearer and more potent the longer they go on.

With "Well, I'm not going to listen," Tom seems to change his action again, threatening to leave. In this third beat, he *forces Amanda to recognize she has gone too far*. He's fed up with his job at Continental Shoemakers and her daily call to rise and shine. Amanda is also at the end of her patience. She *accuses Tom of jeopardizing the family's security*. The following beat probably starts when Amanda grabs at Tom, *demanding to know where he's going*. Notice how so many of the beat changes occur on physical interactions. This makes telling a clear and effective story much simpler.

By the end of the scene, Tom's only way of getting through to Amanda is to *shock or terrify her* with his tall tale of a life of crime. His actions throughout the scene contribute to the objective of *getting her off his back*. Her actions seem designed to *make Tom take responsibility for himself*, so he'll accept his family obligations. These two objectives set up a very direct and explosive conflict, which is bound to energize the scene. We may not have initially recognized that conflict, but specifying actions for each beat has generated a

---

TIP: THE IMPORTANCE OF ACTIONS AND BEATS

Defining actions and locating beats are important aspects of early rehearsals, but you needn't obsess over vocabulary and beat placement. By suggesting more than one choice, I've tried to indicate that there is no single correct action or placement for a scene or beat. The purpose of outlining beats is twofold: to unearth actions and to clarify the story by breaking it into segments. Whenever I stop the actors for some reason, I have them pick up again just before or at the beginning of a new beat. *Rehearsing beat by beat helps instill the beat structure.*

framework of initial beats that we can now use to further develop and refine the scene.

In this early stage of rehearsals, before the director starts taking extensive written notes, discussion is one mode of communicating with actors. But discussion has its limits and pitfalls. When it becomes an intellectual exercise, it disrupts the visceral work that actors must do. Most directors talk too much and spend more time than necessary in discussion. Doing is always more effective than talking. When actors want to talk about a scene, I respond to one of their ideas with "Let's try it." Making this a routine will help actors work more effectively.

You may find it possible—even in the first week of rehearsal—to work through most of the play, roughly outlining the beats and concentrating on the given circumstances—in which case you've made considerable progress in penetrating the play and telling the story. At the same time, you've also probably begun to stage the play—the subject of the next chapter. The chapters that follow outline other aspects of the rehearsal process, many of which occur simultaneously.

REHEARSAL DECORUM

Early rehearsals establish not only the initial explorations of the text but the emotional groundwork for the rehearsal process itself. Rehearsals are more than just business, and actors are not just employees. Creative and imaginative currents inevitably stir emotional behavior and conflict. Directors relate to casts in as many ways as there are directors. The most consistently effective are those that regard actors with respect, tact, and appreciation, as colleagues and members of a team. There are many stories of successful directors who dictate to and intimidate actors. (I know one artistic director who is disinclined to hire directors whom actors enjoy working with, so enamored is he of the director-as-autocrat model.) This may produce a desired effect, but the complete production will usually lack an aspect of the soul or an esprit de corps.

Most directors desire to be liked, but while there is no reason for a director to be cruel, this goal is often at odds with creating art. The confident director doesn't shy away from leadership or pretend that the company is a democracy. At the same time, you'll get the most from your actors if you are flexible, open, and available. If you were on a difficult expedition, you would not want the guide to let everyone vote on the direction to take. By the same token, as an athlete you would expect a coach to elicit your very best, while motivating you to stay the course.

A trusted stage manager can help make the rehearsal process productive and satisfying and should be accorded the same respect due the cast and staff. It's important to meet or talk with the stage manager before rehearsals to discuss your expectations about the procedures and the tenor of rehearsals. As the person in charge of recording the acting, providing rehearsal props and furniture, and communicating with staff and designers, she is crucial to the success of rehearsals. I personally also assign the stage manager to oversee issues such as tardiness, learning lines, and conflicts with rehearsal times so that I don't have to play the role of policeman. The stage manager will also write daily rehearsal reports for the staff and the designers. These reports provide a good indication of how the two of you are communicating.

Because the stage manager is in charge of running the show from technical rehearsals on, I try to involve her as much as possible. She should understand the reasoning behind the choices the actors and director make, since she may be the person to put a replacement actor into the production. She can also act as a sounding board when problems arise and gauge the progress and atmosphere of rehearsals. Stage managers—even professionals—vary from those who seem distracted or uncommitted to those who are always one step ahead, asking timely questions, making sure they understand the director's intentions, and acting as communications director during rehearsals.

Rarely will a director meet with no resistance from a cast. I always welcome actors to respectfully challenge ideas to determine their effectiveness. But when an actor spends more time disputing the director than working on the role, it's time to have a private talk. The great majority of conflicts can be resolved, but if an actor seems unable to work constructively with you or the other actors, it's much better—for the actor and for the production—for that person to be released immediately.

Two common behaviors that should be nipped in the bud are actors trying to direct other actors and actors asking their partners to facilitate their own work. An actor who tells another actor "I need you to do x so that I can do y" misunderstands and distrusts the acting process. No actor should presume to know what another actor needs or tell another how a scene should be played. Not only does it infringe on the work of the other, but an actor who knows what his partner will do has eliminated any chance of spontaneity. Trial and error, give and take, are the ways to generate exciting acting.

Another potential pitfall is stressing process over results. No matter how much a director wants to be the leader of a beloved community of artists, rehearsals are a means to an end: the artistic product. Audiences do not get to see the process, and they wouldn't have much interest in it if they could. Rehearsals should be imaginative, creative, and playful, but ultimately their purpose is to build a production that others will pay to see.

The thinking and strategies presented in this chapter represent only one aspect of a director's perspective in rehearsals. The other side—attending to the play's structural elements—is discussed in Chapter 12. Although I've separated the two points of view for the purposes of clarity, in practice they work together. I start rehearsals by helping actors construct the life of the characters through action. I do this for many reasons, not the least of which is that it's easier to work on structure once the action becomes visible. And if there are actors who cannot play basic actions or endow circumstances authentically, you had better know sooner rather than later. Eliciting truthful acting is the sine qua non of early rehearsals.

ALTERNATIVE PROCESSES

Every director has a unique way of working. Mine is to start by using the language of action to elicit behavior; others work primarily with physical images and movement. With the latter approach, action and intention theoretically emerge from exploring the physical side of characters, and hopefully the actors provide the necessary internal reality.

One such movement-based approach is Viewpoints, which its creators define as a way of naming basic principles of movement, generating staging and composition, and training performers. Highlighting space, movement, and rhythm, it largely excludes the work of constructing the internal reality of a character. In its purest form, Viewpoints presumes that performance can be accessed entirely through external means, or that actors will create inner life on their own.

Unquestionably, an awareness of tempo, shape, gesture, and spatial relationships—four of the nine viewpoints—is essential to performing and directing. Though most actors possess some spatial and kinetic sensitivity, Viewpoints would seem to be an effective antidote to an overreliance on emotion or intellect. Any approach that stimulates a different way of looking at a text is beneficial for actors and directors.

To my mind, Viewpoints becomes problematic when it is used as the *exclusive* technique for acting and directing. Clever movements and pretty pictures then become the raison d'être of production, as only the surface of a text is played. A number of troupes claiming allegiance to this method turn out productions that are showy but hollow, soulless exercises in presentational theater. The actors wear their performances like overcoats, with little perceptible relationship between the human being and the performance. And staging takes precedence over the text. Ironically, a technique intended to heighten one's awareness of bodies in space often winds up producing disembodied performances.

Some directors make judicious use of some of the basic principles, integrating them into a full exploration of character and language. But others employ Viewpoints as the primary rehearsal method rather than as a training and compositional tool. Some go so far as to use rehearsals to train actors. They call out one of the Viewpoints and the cast is asked to react physically, not to the text, but to the concept.

It isn't surprising that even fervent advocates of Viewpoints report resistance from actors who find the training "too much 'like school.' " Less didactic adherents of the method, such as director Scott Zigler, find it to be a useful resource as long as intellectual concepts aren't interposed between the actor and the text:

> I would suggest that any technique should be used unconsciously and not consciously. If everyone is sitting around talking about the technique that they are using in rehearsal, for me something has already lost its way a little bit. If you are sitting around in scene work talking about which Viewpoints am I going to use here, that, to me, is a mistaken application of the theory as much as if you were sitting around going, "What affective memory am I going to use here?" My understanding of training is that you train in a theory so your ability to bring it to bear in rehearsal becomes unconscious.

Like certain techniques of postmodern dance (such as contact improvisation), Viewpointing can generate staging and even serve as the basis for developing an entire performance "text." When a previously scripted play is rehearsed, however, movement and text are sometimes set in opposition to each other: in one type of Viewpointing process, staging is generated first, and the text is later put on top of the movement, with the result that the movement is a critique of the text. The clear intention is to expose the disjunction between physical and verbal behavior. The tone of these productions is exclusively ironic, as script and staging are literally alienated from each other. Devised by a choreographer, Viewpointing by itself tends to devalue language and attempts, at times, to prove its inadequacy. But most plays do not communicate the discrepancy between language and movement. Using only Viewpoints to rehearse language-oriented plays would seem to be virtually impossible.

One of the chief attractions of Viewpoints is that it makes rehearsing a more democratic process. For instance, actors learn to create some of their own staging. A director calls out "Spatial relationship!" and the actors should be able to, in the words of one of its practitioners, "adjust accordingly to create a more 'readable' stage picture." But most directors will surely recognize that a clear and balanced composition isn't necessarily an illuminating one. Staging and composition have to serve the telling of a story, or the choices become arbitrary and the production will lack coherence.

The ideas and practices described in this book do not prescribe or require a single way of working. Not surprisingly, the most successful directors develop a personal technique through trial and error. A flexible, continually evolving method, rather than a closed system, is, to my mind, the best way of suiting the method to a particular project.

REHEARSING A NEW PLAY

All of the work covered in this chapter pertains to directing any type of play, but new plays present additional challenges and obligations. When a playwright is present and the script is in flux through much of the rehearsal process, all the director's skills will be called upon to mediate between text, actors, and author. Because it generally takes longer in rehearsals for a new play to emerge, a special quotient of patience and courage is required to direct them.

In this situation, perhaps the most difficult issue a director faces is deciding whether a problem should be solved by the playwright or by the actors and director. My inclination is to test a number of different tacks in rehearsal before asking the author to consider rewriting. While a savvy playwright will know when to accommodate a production, the basic integrity of the play should never be sacrificed. It is the director's formidable job to balance the demands of the play with a sense of what will serve a production.

The director can help the process along, I believe, by getting the entire play on its feet as soon as is feasible. My strategy is to work toward a full "stumble-through" about halfway through the rehearsal period. This gives the playwright a view of the whole play, enabling her to make broader and more informed decisions about what works and what needs to be revised. Delaying a run-through until late in rehearsals will forfeit an early chance to see problems in the play's overall shape and structure.

A playwright's presence in rehearsals can be enormously valuable. I try to persuade the writer to stay in residence through much of the first week, to develop an agenda for revisions, answer questions, and offer the kind of personal background that is often stimulating and exciting for a cast. With the playwright in attendance in this early phase, actors can test the revisions immediately. Once staging and more intensive explorations begin, I encourage the playwright to allow the actors and myself to work alone, usually for at least a week. A fundamental principle of the rehearsal process is that it rarely if ever proceeds in a straight line. It's vital to work slowly and at tangents that may seem useless and even counterproductive to an author. Just as a detective investigates a case from several angles, rehearsals are most productive when they examine a play from different directions.

Occasionally, a playwright will want to stay for an entire rehearsal period. My experience is that his constant presence may inhibit the actors and director, placing subtle pressure on them to be accurate instead of taking the risks that are so often needed to make exciting discoveries. A playwright's hiatus from rehearsals also gives actors and directors a break from concentrating on rewrites and the chance to sharpen the existing text. In new play production, constantly introducing revisions into rehearsals is a common mistake, because it never allows the actors and director to catch their creative breaths.

I normally ask the playwright to return for the first stumble-through of the entire play and, if possible, to be present through previews. The period between the first run-through and the performances is a good time for writer and director to take stock of the play and consider a second stage of revisions if needed. By the time previews begin, major revisions should have already been inserted. Previews are essential to producing a new play, which, if it is in its premiere, the writer and director have never seen in front of an audience. A preview period that is long enough may afford time to try out new scenes. But at a reasonable point before opening, the script should be frozen so that the actors can solidify their performances.

The success of a new play process depends almost entirely on the experience of the playwright and the director. I doubt I could have directed my first new play with any confidence had I not already assisted other directors and witnessed their work. New playwrights are sometimes either too eager to change their plays or so anxious they do not trust rehearsals as a basis for revisions. More experienced authors *rely* on rehearsals to complete their understanding of what they have written. When I directed *The Road to Nirvana* by Arthur Kopit, two productions of the play were in rehearsal at different theaters at the same time. The play had already had its premiere, but the playwright was eager to revise. What was remarkable was Kopit's ability to respond to different casts and directors. Shuttling between two theaters, computer in tow, he managed to write two (slightly different) versions of the play.

The experience of working on a new play can be very rewarding when director and author trust each other and the process.

TEN

STAGING

G lancing through a widely read directing textbook from the middle of the last century reveals just how much the job and the training have changed. *Fundamentals of Play Directing* dealt mostly with staging, presenting it as a technical process of composition separate from interpretation or acting. This chapter treats composition as an aspect of staging and staging as a product of eliciting actions and telling a story.

Even before blocking begins, some of it will have already been determined—or at least influenced—by the ground plan, which has established the entrances and exits, the playing areas, and their relationship to the stage space. Then if the actors are intensively pursuing objectives by playing actions with significant physical activity, even more staging should emerge naturally. This doesn't mean a play stages itself, especially with less experienced actors. But to my mind, staging should start as an attempt to create behavior by underlining the action, elucidating the given circumstances, and developing the relationships.

First, to clarify terms, *blocking* denotes the positioning and movement of the actors. *Staging* is often synonymous with *blocking*, while *composition* entails the visual imagery created by the combination of staging and design. I use *activity* to define specific physical tasks, such as lighting a cigarette, reading a book, or sewing. Activities may reinforce the action or operate independently, though they are often used to punctuate beat changes. *Business* refers to activities tied to props.

TIP: WHEN TO BLOCK

Ideally, movement and activity evolve while you are exploring the given circumstances and testing various actions. If I were an actor, I'd feel restricted by immediate blocking (unless I had only limited experience). Blocking conceived entirely by the director prior to rehearsals for the purposes of developing the ground plan, while sometimes useful, cannot capture the complex reality of actors onstage.

Because I regard actors as full collaborators in the process of physicalizing the play, I rarely dictate blocking when they have just gotten onto their feet. As I've developed as a director, I've found it much more creative, natural, and productive to integrate blocking into the early discovery rehearsals, allowing experienced actors to explore the space and their physical impulses the first few times through a scene. Since not all actors are adept at doing this, you should be ready to help those who need immediate blocking. Some circumstances warrant early blocking (such as lack of time or actor experience), but I prefer to think that the mingling of actors' and director's insights produces a more textured result than would the director's alone. I doubt that actors respect a director any less for not hard-blocking the play immediately. In my experience, most relish the freedom to experiment.

Once actors have begun to test their physical impulses, I suggest—in addition to actions—movements designed to reinforce or alter their playing. Sometimes a physical prompt that implies an action is the most potent direction. Instead of verbalizing an action or telling an actor to explore the relationship with his scene partner, I might simply ask him to sit down on a bench very close to her. This allows the actor to figure out the action and the impact of the move himself.

Seasoned actors will usually recognize these suggestions, not as final staging, but as exploratory physical cues for stimulating action and enhancing relationships. Whether or not you rely on actors to develop the initial blocking ideas, you should still have given thought to where each scene is to be played, the physicalizing of key moments, and how relationships might be clarified through movement. With less experienced actors, it's wise to rough in blocking almost as soon as they are on their feet, to allow them to concentrate on playing action rather than worry about where they should be.

Unless we have spent more than a couple of days at the table, by the end of the first week I have usually outlined a simple beat structure and a rudimentary staging for most, if not all, of the play in just a little more time than if we had concentrated entirely on blocking. Moreover, the staging we've accomplished is tied to our discoveries about the action. Though the blocking is bound to change, I ask the stage manager to record all of the various versions in case we want to utilize an old move later on. As rehearsals progress, we will continue to invent activities and business that reinforce the action and that give variety and texture to the behavior. Except when visual imagery is the predominant element in a production, a director who begins staging by creating pretty pictures will very likely short-circuit the exploration of action and behavior.

Realistic plays tend to be both easier and more complex to stage. To some extent, the set pieces that represent an actual space dictate movement and activities. Characters tend to move from one prop or furniture piece to another—or to another character. This grounds the staging in everyday behavior but also demands a meticulous attention to detail. In scene 3 of *The Glass Menagerie*, much of the staging after Tom's monologue is implicit in the dialogue. Tom's "Now what are you up to?" indicates that Amanda has moved toward him from the telephone. And the line "I'm trying to save your eyesight" signals her business with the lamp. In nonrealistic plays, much less staging is implied by the lines. Although still related to behavior, movement becomes a more symbolic expression of the changing dynamics of action and relationship.

Regardless of a play's style, one way to ensure that the staging reinforces the action (unless there is a special reason to contradict it) is to punctuate each new beat with business, activity, or movement. Then whenever actions change they will be underlined by some physicalization. Movement thus becomes the grammar of storytelling. This accomplishes two things: it helps the audience understand where the story changes, and at the same time it inculcates in the actors the play's beat structure.

TIP: USING THE TURN

A definitive turn by one actor toward another is often enough to mark a beat change, especially in plays where characters aren't moving from one sit-down location to another. Though it may seem like micromanaging, to highlight a critical moment you may need to be involved in determining the timing of a turn. In film the look is an even more important gesture: it's often used to cover a cut from one shot to another.

Whether you block loosely or precisely, the staging must be purposeful. When actors start to wander, it indicates they're not sure of what they're doing (i.e., what action to play or why). The acting becomes generalized, and the stage picture—designed to help tell the story—becomes muddy. Some less experienced actors make a habit of moving closer to the other actor whenever they speak, as if force or emphasis required greater proximity. Closeness between actors onstage is normally saved for intense, passionate moments. If the position is held too long, the stage picture will feel static and anticlimactic.

One of the keys to creating convincing stage behavior is having an instinct about the way proximity (and body language) relates to specific situations. For instance, powerful actions and speeches usually require substantial physical space; staging actors too close together in such scenes will often smother their actions. Experienced actors often possess a radar about action, proximity, and relationship, but sometimes a director will need to modify their instincts to achieve the appropriate distance and physicality. Can intimate moments be played between two actors on opposite sides of a room? Probably not. What about moments of encouraging, goading, enticing, or commanding? While there is no correct physical relationship for a particular action, all good staging justifies the arrangement of actors to effectively express action and relationship.

Nor is there is a formula as to how much movement a play can sustain. Language plays, such as those by Shakespeare, Shaw, or Wilde, can handle far less movement than realistic ones, in which behavior is nearly as prominent as language. It's difficult for an audience to assimilate poetry or complex language when there is constant movement. The same is true of comedy. Stillness and a full-face position are often needed for the audience to absorb a punch line or gag. It's often better to start with less staging than more. For instance, when one actor leaves a pairing, explore the possible value in maintaining the new arrangement before you have the stationary actor join the one who moved.

COMPOSITION

In this chapter I assume that, like a young painter who possesses a visual instinct, you have some sensitivity to composition. In fact, it may very well be impossible to teach this awareness from scratch.

By studying the principles of composition through visual art, a painter can build acuity, but a director, like a sculptor, can truly master compositional skills only by continually working in three dimensions.

At some point, it's certainly worthwhile to try out the images that occurred to you during your preparation. Since staging automatically creates pictures, they should contribute to the narrative. When a play's compositions are precise, someone who is hearing disabled should be able to understand most of the story. Not every moment of a production has to have a beautiful picture, but one way to frame a key moment and imprint it in the audience's mind is to compose an arresting image.

Achieving precise and visually evocative stage pictures depends, to a great extent, on creating effective focus. (This is more complicated in stage directing than in film, where the camera lens does much of the work.) For an image to be compelling, the audience must know how to look at it. Focus provides the code. It can be realized through placement, movement, voice, lighting, and costume.

When staging is the primary factor, an actor is highlighted most easily by moving upstage of his partner, who must normally turn back to him to speak or listen (Figure 1). This configuration, in which the audience sees the full figure of Actor 1, is generally used when Actor 1 is the key player. The featured character doesn't always have to occupy an upstage

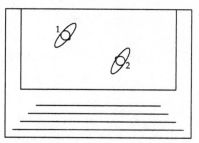

Figure 1 — Actor 1 is in a stronger (upstage) position than Actor 2.

position, and many shared moments are best composed with the actors in profile facing each other on the same plane. But I am always amazed at how often directors violate the upstage principle, putting the prominent actor in the weaker (Actor 2) position and thereby dissipating the impact of a moment. If taking an upstage position weren't an important principle of focus, actors would never "cheat" upstage—as they sometimes do—to take the focus from their partners. The principle pertains not only to proscenium or end-staging but also to thrust (three-quarter) configurations.

There are other ways to make Actor 1 the dominant figure.

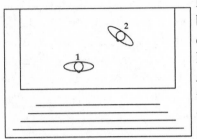

Putting him downstage of Actor 2 but looking out toward the audience draws the focus on him (if he's speaking), no matter where Actor 2 is standing. If Actor 2 is turned toward Actor 1, the focus will be even clearer (Figure 2). Relative positions and body levels are also important in establishing focus. A standing actor is likely to have greater focus than one who is sitting, just as an actor on a platform will be seen more easily than one on the floor.

Figure 2 — Actor 1 is downstage but looking out toward the audience—and is thus in the stronger position.

Another critical principle of composition is balance. Any imbalance should be used deliberately to express change or instability; otherwise it will seem purposeless. In most well-staged productions, much of the play happens in or near a large central area of the set. When it doesn't, the audience feels as if they are on a ship that is listing. There's no reason to center the entire play, but the eye instinc-

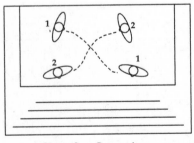

tively gives more importance and weight to the middle of a picture. Consistently staging key moments substantially off-center can decrease their impact. Balance is also the principle behind *countering*, in which one actor rebalances the stage in response to a partner who has moved in front of or behind him. (Visualize an X created by the two movements; see Figure 3.) But too much countering becomes tedious. The audience inherently needs to see most of

Figure 3 — Countering.

the stage used, and in different ways. Variety is crucial to composition, as it is to all aspects of directing.

Some textbooks argue that certain areas on a proscenium stage have an absolute value or weight. While center stage is, as I've pointed out, a potentially powerful place, effective moments can be staged in other locations depending on how much focus they're given. Some years ago, when I was interviewing for a job teaching directing, an elderly professor asked me where onstage I would place an actor if I wanted her to be seen as late as possible when the curtain rose. I knew the answer he wanted was "down left" (the lower right part of the stage from an audience's perspective). A Western audience reads the stage from left to right, so that an actor positioned down left would be noticed last. In practice, I replied, a director can delay an actor's appearance in any number of ways, with scenery, lighting, change of body position, or movement. A wide frown signaled his disapproval, but in my youthful impetuousness, I wanted him to know that I thought the question was theoretical. Because a director works with bodies in motion, the laws of composition are quite fluid, especially compared to two-dimensional objects such as paintings.

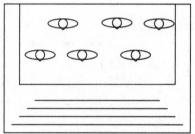

Figure 4 — Staging in triangles utilizes diagonals.

Composition has several axioms. Diagonals are generally more dynamic than straight lines because they infuse both movement and composition with greater energy. This is why scenes with three characters are more effectively staged in triangles than in straight lines. No matter which way the triangle faces, there are at least two diagonal lines (Figure 4). And using a set piece as a physical obstacle between two actors can add significant tension to a moment.

But a director can learn only so much about the technical principles of composition from diagrams. Like most other artistic endeavors, the ability to stage a play matures with experience. A developing director can pick up more about composition by observing the paintings of the Renaissance masters than by memorizing the rules of optics. Of course, nothing substitutes for trying out staging ideas with live actors.

DIFFERENT STAGE SPACES

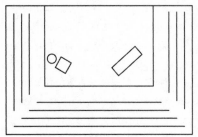

Figure 5 — Set pieces anchor the downstage corners.

Staging in thrust and arena theaters is considerably more complicated than staging in proscenium or open stages. In a thrust, with the audience on three sides, the set can be oriented to stimulate diagonal movement so that the actors are seen from many angles. Major scenic elements must play upstage so as not to block the audiences on the extreme sides. It's usually advantageous to anchor the downstage corners (at the *vomitoria*, or downstage entrances) with simple set pieces to encourage a diagonal traffic flow (Figure 5). If actors are too close to one another, even on a diagonal, there will not be enough angles of vision for the audience to see into the grouping. The physical closeness of actors must be carefully orchestrated and saved for decisive moments, or played well upstage (just beyond where the seats on either side end).

In thrust, a "50-50" position—two actors facing each other in profile on the same horizontal plane—is problematic unless they're both upstage. That's because if they're in a straight line, they will actually block each other from the side seating areas (Figure 6). This means the principle of placing the main speaker in an upstage position is even more important than on a proscenium stage. Staging in thrust demands more movement than on a proscenium, since keeping the featured character in the stronger position as often as possible requires a lot of trading of downstage and upstage positions.

Since 50-50 arrangements are less effective in thrust, it's useful to scout for ways that actors can "play out," facing the audience—so that most of the audience can see both faces in a two-person scene. One way to do this is to establish an imaginary fourth-wall window or a vista beyond the audience, through

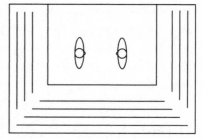

Figure 6 — Actors in a 50-50 position block each other on a thrust stage.

which the actors can look. Another strategy is to place a seated actor in a downstage corner so that she can "open up" a more centrally located actor to much of the audience (Figure 7). Although an actor in a downstage corner is visible to most audience members in thrust, many directors overestimate this location. There's nothing wrong with staging in corners, but important two-person scenes played there may not register strongly enough.

As on a thrust stage, when there is audience on four sides, considerable movement is necessary. A rule of thumb is that every audience member should be able

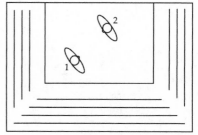

Figure 7 — Actor 1 opens up Actor 2.

to see at least one actor's face at all times. To make sure each section doesn't see the *same* actor's face for too long, you'll need to justify actors changing sides often. Putting set pieces in the corners (and other entrances or seating divisions) helps point actors toward the center and cuts down on the number of audience members to whom the actor's back is turned. Set pieces placed in the middle of the stage must be skeletal (or backless) so that opposite sections of audience can see completely across the stage. And diagonals can be encouraged by situating pieces at right angles (Figure 8).

Although composition is an important aspect of staging, it must

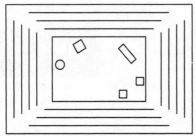

Figure 8 — Set pieces are placed in an
arena configuration.

support the story and punctuate changes of action, or it will
seem arbitrary and confusing to
actors and audiences alike. In the
most productive rehearsal methods, staging, composing, and acting become integrated into a
single process.

ELEVEN

THE MIDDLE REHEARSALS:
PROBLEM SOLVING

P utting into place a framework of action and staging in the early phases of a production allows you to spend the middle period of rehearsals strengthening the action, amplifying character and relationship, and solving specific problems. Once the story emerges, its structure can be refined. This chapter presents a series of questions and strategies designed to sharpen the acting, while the next chapter is devoted to shaping the story.

APPROACHING MIDDLE REHEARSALS

I take a more leisurely pace in the middle rehearsals, spending longer periods on each scene to investigate key moments and dig deeper for the ambiguities. At this stage, I tend to stop the work right away if, for example, a key circumstance at the beginning of a beat is missed, or actions seem impractical (unless we're investigating an entirely new path). Feeding direction while a scene is being played—known as *side coaching*—can be effective, especially with less experienced actors. As often as possible, once the beats become clear, I let the actors run together a number of beats, or even a scene, to begin to capture the play's ebb and flow. One of my major goals in rehearsal is to facilitate the actor's ongoing life as the character.

In the middle rehearsals, most beginning directors tend to allow actors too few repetitions to absorb the direction. Of course, too many repetitions of a play's most passionate moments can dry out actors. But sometimes a director has to be able to concede that a certain problem cannot be solved immediately. It's far more productive to admit ignorance or a temporary lack of inspiration, and move on, than dig in one's heels and force a result. Whether deliberately or not, you will already have set a routine for working with the actors, which you should look to adjust, when necessary.

TIP: SCHEDULING

Although in community theater it is common practice to map out in advance an entire rehearsal schedule, it's rarely done in the profession and shouldn't be practiced at any level. Any estimate done before rehearsals of which scenes will need the most work will continually change over the course of the process, because it's virtually impossible to forecast the pace of discovery and each actor's development. Episodic plays tend to need more rehearsal time than plays with just a few major scenes, because each time the actors begin a scene, a different set of given circumstances is in effect. Aside from setting a target date for the first run-through, I try not to announce the schedule of scene work more than a day or two in advance, subject to conflicts. Well before the actors arrive, however, I construct a skeletal hypothetical schedule to make sure there is sufficient time for each stage of the process and to earmark, in coordination with the theater, the days of work and rest for each week and the technical rehearsals.

As rehearsals proceed, I like to have an assistant or a

stage manager keep a flow chart of how often and how long a scene has been worked. This makes scheduling future days much easier and reminds me to allot time for each scene. While it might seem absurdly obvious to advise that at this stage you rehearse those scenes and moments that need to be fixed, you would be surprised to find how many directors overrehearse scenes that are already working and disregard the trouble spots.

DEEPENING THE ACTION

Even if you have set up strong conflicts of playable actions for a particular scene, when you return to it after a day or two, you may find the actors either don't recall or can't justify what they originally played. Questioning choices is a natural process; it also occurs because actors are trying to link moments together in greater detail. You may need to revisit the given circumstances, rethink choices of action, or upgrade them. An actor whose effort *to gain forgiveness* doesn't bring results would probably be more successful with a stronger action, such as—if the circumstances permit—*pleading for her life*. Assessing the playability of actions is a continual directorial concern. For example, the action *to explicate* is less forceful than the action *to lay it on the line*, just as *to support* is more concrete than *to corroborate*. When actions are too general, not potent enough, or too intellectual, the acting is usually ineffective.

Sometimes asking the question "in order to . . . ?" will elicit a more forceful action by making an actor aware of a larger goal. For instance, an actor who cannot understand why her character must deflect her mother's criticism might be reminded that it serves the goal of standing on her own two feet. And asking what character x wants from character y will often crack open a scene that seems intractable. When a scene continues to stall, actors may be able to reconnect by sitting down at a table and playing the scene once quietly to each other. This releases them from the old blocking, the obligation to immediately invent new movement, and some of the previous acting choices.

GIVE-AND-TAKE

When an actor's response to a partner is consistently ineffective, your first impulse might be to redirect that actor. But much of the time the problem lies with the partner, the one triggering the reaction. At this stage, when give-and-take is stymied, it's wise to reinforce the initiating action rather than moderate the response. Otherwise, the reactor will be forced into false responses, and the exploratory process of testing actions will be stalled. A cardinal rule of acting is to take what you are given. Another is, exact a response—don't expect or require it. In scene 3 of *The Glass Menagerie*, if the actor playing Amanda isn't really challenging the actor playing Tom to admit his depravity, he shouldn't pretend that she is. In other words, he shouldn't play *to get her off his back once and for all* if she really doesn't compel it. Just because the text says a character needs to do something, doesn't mean a responding actor should do it if it isn't a truthful reaction. It's better, at least once, to have the responding actor disregard the text until the dynamic between the two actors allows the action the text describes to occur naturally. This will be difficult for many actors and directors, but it can help actors play truthfully. It's a technique, however, that will succeed only if it's done in a cooperative spirit. Later in the process, it becomes the reactor's responsibility to find something in the partner's playing that generates a truthful reaction.

Similarly, when a transition between beats seems rote or stale, the solution usually lies not in the text but in the actor exchange. Amanda's transition from making Laura face the future to encouraging her to reestablish a relationship with Jim occurs, ostensibly, because of Laura's memory of a high school infatuation. But the textual explanation alone does not justify the transition. The actor playing Amanda might be compelled by the other actor's smile or her eyes or the change in her voice when she speaks of Jim. It's an actor's job to ground transitions in the moment-to-moment interaction with a part-

ner. When this doesn't occur, it's up to the director to recommend a
way to enliven the transition.

Every good production operates on three levels simultaneously:
text, subtext, and actor interplay. Productions that lack spontaneous
interaction rarely succeed on the first two levels. Each night brings a
new audience and the need for actors to base their work on the
moment-to-moment reality of that performance. To understand
the importance of spontaneity, consider how distracted an audience
would be if a glass accidentally broke onstage and the actors chose to
ignore it.

Like everyone else, actors fall into patterns, which makes dialogue stale. One strategy for refreshing the interchanges is to encourage incorporating the tics, hesitations, and overlaps of everyday
speech. Freeing actors to explore the texture of real conversation will
often revive their interaction. (This works well with relatively realistic
plays but causes problems with more language-driven material.)

At times even the best actors must be reminded to talk and listen.
But, you may ask, haven't they been doing that all along? Not necessarily. Some actors are prone to speechify instead of talk; others gaze
at their scene partners but don't really listen. One can hear without
listening, as we often do when we're occupied with another activity. I
define listening as active behavior involving hearing, absorbing, and

TIP: PROMOTING TALKING AND LISTENING

To get young actors to improve their talking and listening,
have them state each other's real names before speaking or
ask them to repeat the partner's last line before they say
theirs.

Another exercise requires actors to voice a thought (an
inner monologue), related to the other actor or character,
prior to each line. The intention behind these exercises is
to break up habitual patterns and stimulate spontaneity.

deciphering the other person's intentions. You may be able to help an actor listen just by reminding him what another actor has just said or done. The same holds true for a speaker: if a moment doesn't work, the actor may not really be "landing" the action on her partner. The words should be a fishing line, with the speaker making sure the listener is hooked. Some actors refer to this as "taking the other actor's temperature"—meaning not only playing an action but measuring its impact.

When an actor cannot commit to a moment, personalization is usually the issue. Even very skilled actors have moments in a script with which they cannot easily identify. In that situation, a director can assist without resorting to psychoanalysis or Method techniques. Relating to an extreme act, such as murder, requires an actor to imagine or consider a comparable act. A director should be able to offer, if needed, an analogy, an "as if." For instance, for a particular actor, abandoning one's family might be emotionally equivalent to committing murder. As always, you must find strategies for the individual actor rather than using a one-size-fits-all approach. Instead of an "as if," you can ask the question formulated by Vakhtangov, one of Stanislavski's peers: "What would make you, in similar circumstances, do what your character does?" The question assumes that we all have within us the capacity to produce most human behavior, and it engages an actor's imagination, not just his personal experience.

IMPROVISATION

Though all rehearsing is in effect improvising, the term usually denotes a structured situation built around a "who, what, or where" assumption. Yet despite its potential, actors may have qualms about using improvisation. It often connotes the rehearsed, over-the-top routines of mediocre comedians and comedy troupes. Some directors have also given it a bad name by using it indiscriminately or basing it on circumstances that are radically different from those of the play. Asking an actor to play a giraffe may be fine for a class, but it has its limits in rehearsal. When I think an improvisation might help, I never actually mention the word. I'll simply say, "Let's start the scene with this circumstance." Actors who are free enough can benefit greatly from more extended improvising.

Let's say the actor playing Laura can't imagine her character relating to the Gentleman Caller. An improvisation between her and the actor playing the Gentleman Caller, based on a specific situation in their past, might unlock her imagination. Proposing a scene that is implied by or left out of a script is also an effective way of setting up an improvisation. Another is to create a different given circumstance for a scene. If the actor playing Tom wants even less to do with Amanda than scene 3 requires, what would happen if his character really does have something to hide? Perhaps he hasn't just been going to the movies. Maybe he's been spending time at a brothel or a bar with a questionable reputation. Playing or improvising the scene with that new circumstance would produce a very different reaction when Amanda accuses him of jeopardizing the family's security.

THE PASSOVER QUESTION

Nothing can sap an actor's energy faster than playing behavior as if it is habitual. One antidote is to concentrate on the uniqueness of a scene. On the Jewish holiday of Passover, a question is asked, "Why is this night different from all others?" This is more or less the question a director must ask of every scene: "How is this scene different from all others?" The answer should inspire more compelling acting because first-time experiences are inherently exciting to actors and audiences. This point is so critical that, even if you have started your rehearsals by exploring this question, you may need to raise it again. Why is scene 2 of *The Glass Menagerie* different from all others? After all, it can't be the first time Amanda has extolled the virtues of finding a husband. But it is the first time Amanda has caught Laura lying and failing to go to school. This is proof that Laura's future is in jeopardy. It's also the first time Laura has talked about a boy she liked in high school. No wonder Amanda is hopeful at the end of the scene. The first-time experience of each scene is one of the keys to unlocking the energy of a play.

Another source of energy is making a discovery. Think of what happens when a cartoon character suddenly has an idea: a light bulb appears over her head. The discovery that drives scene 2 of *The Glass Menagerie* occurs when Amanda learns of Laura's crush on a boy in high school. At the beginning of *Nora*, Torvald's discovery that Nora has been shopping catapults the first scene forward. Discoveries are very often turning points. So important is Amanda's discovery that it dramatically alters her emotional state, paving the way for a new optimism and a new direction for the scene. Giving an actor a secret about a scene can also be an effective way to energize her and her interaction with her partner.

STAKES

Harnessing a first-time experience makes a situation arousing, unique, and unrepeatable — and it inevitably raises the stakes. I think of stakes as *the consequences for each character of achieving or failing to achieve a superobjective*. For Amanda, the stakes for failing to provide for the family's future is the death of the family. For Tom, the stakes of establishing his independence may be his soul. The stakes for the major characters in Shakespeare's dramas are almost always life and death, which is partly what makes them so compelling. Losing sight of the stakes is common at various points in the rehearsal process, and reconnecting with them is a primary means of recharging the acting without resorting to vague directives like "It needs to be more intense." When the stakes have already been discussed but seem less than compelling, raise them. One way is to give an actor a "clock." Make her aware there is a time limit on achieving the objective. What is the clock for Amanda? Laura will not always be young, and if she doesn't start soon, she may never find a husband. You can create other improvisations to intensify the stakes by inventing various conditions and constraints. It's usually in the middle period of rehearsals that a director will need to remind some actors of how urgently they need to achieve their objectives.

THE WATERGATE QUESTION

Sometimes a lack of animation is the result of an actor assuming something that the character doesn't know. When this happens, the actor feels little need to pursue the character's goals, and less need translates into less energy. Urging the actor to "be more energetic" can breed generalized acting. Experienced directors can often tell what actors are assuming. But no one's perception is flawless, which is why when a director or an actor isn't sure of what the character should know or assume, it's worth taking time to discuss it. The question prosecutors of the 1970s Watergate scandal asked of the accused is what the actor (and director) must ask of a character: "What did he know, and when did he know it?" A related axiom: Always assume, until you discover otherwise, that a character is asking a question in order to find an answer.

A scene from *Nora* provides a clear example. Krogstad, who secretly loaned Nora the money to pay for Torvald's life-saving vacation, has come to ask her to intercede on his behalf so that he can keep his job at the bank that Torvald manages. Fearing he may be laid off, Krogstad threatens to tell Torvald of the loan. Nora refuses to be threatened, telling Krogstad that if her husband does find out, he would support her efforts and pay the loan back immediately. Krogstad points out a problem: the date and her father's signature on the agreement (as a guarantee of the loan) appear to be in two different styles of writing. He theorizes merely that the contract was backdated, but Nora turns the tables by admitting that she forged her father's signature.

Bergman's cutting of Ibsen's scene has made Krogstad a more sympathetic figure, a man terrified of losing his job. But even in *Nora* (and especially in *A Doll's House*), Krogstad could be played as a villain, which would make the play far less complex and engaging. If Krogstad already knows the father's signature is fake, then he is really only threatening Nora. But if he suspects that only the date, not the signature, is false, he himself is in jeopardy. He has already made a mistake that cost him his original profession; if whoever advanced him the money were to find out that Nora forged the signature, it would mean his undoing. So instead of *toying* with Nora (an action with little at stake) about something he knows, he is actually *begging* her to tell him that the signature was indeed her father's. The stakes are much higher for him, and it's much easier to understand and sympathize with his plight.

MAKING USE OF OBSTACLES

As I mentioned in Chapter 3, obstacles provide the friction against which actions are played. Without them, characters would have no difficulty in achieving their objectives. In a strong, direct conflict, the actions of one character operate as the obstacles for the other, and if actors are truly playing off each other, they will be in touch with most of the pertinent external obstacles. What happens in moments that lack direct conflict? This is when internal obstacles become useful.

For most actors, taking an action down a notch is usually a relatively simple process. A more common problem is lackluster commitment to an action. Working with internal obstacles is a possible remedy. Alerting an actor to the internal forces that are working against his actions can generate a greater struggle on his part, making the scene more arresting for both actor and audience. Toward the end of scene 3 of *The Glass Menagerie*, Tom complains bitterly about his job, and when Amanda tries to physically keep him in the apartment, he unleashes a fantastical tirade about his supposed gangland connections, designed to scare, shock, and outrage Amanda. To have any effect on her, the speech has to be somewhat frightening. She doesn't have to believe he's a mob killer, but she must fear that he is doing something more dangerous at night than going to the movies. Otherwise, her stakes are very low, and she would have no reason to be disturbed.

These are external obstacles for Tom's speech. Internally, he must feel some guilt about his behavior toward Amanda. She is a single mother, desperately trying to hold the family together. His father has already abandoned the family, and he knows she worries about what he does at night. (He apologizes to her in the next scene.) Does this mean the speech should be hesistant? Not necessarily (though the obstacle could be used to modulate Tom's outburst). Working against the obstacle of his guilt, Tom could be *more* enraged—and more frightening—at being the slave of the family.

Nearly every character has a primary internal obstacle—a wound—that is linked to their overall intention. Digging deeper into a character involves recognizing and experimenting with the deficit from which he or she is operating. Amanda's wounds are several and powerful: her husband left his family behind, and she no longer has the comfort of the Southern gentility in which she grew up. Any ac-

TIP: PLAYING OPPOSITES

Discussing an obstacle with an actor may not always produce the desired result. Actions are playable, but obstacles are not; they can only modify the action. A more direct way of accessing an obstacle is to turn it into an action. An actor who must reveal a lack of self-respect as his character's obstacle could play as an action *to punish or sabotage himself.* That kind of experiment tends to inform future repetitions of the scene when he returns to playing the original action.

Turning an obstacle into an action is one example of "playing opposites"—a very good way of bringing out different sides to any behavior. Playing the opposite of what appears to be the obvious action—even if it seems inappropriate—can introduce new colors and even new actions. Conceiving of at least two ways to play a scene will make it easier to suggest opposites in rehearsal.

tor playing the role would need to be in touch with and perhaps reminded of these circumstances.

Obstacles can also be a directorial tool for compensating for an actor's strengths or weaknesses. When an actor doesn't think a partner's action poses a threat, the partner's action can be strengthened. But if this does not work, suggesting an inner obstacle can give friction and intensity to the first actor's work. Utilizing internal obstacles often makes the difference between a very good production—where action and obstacle are in constant tension—and a mediocre one. The characters are richer, and the story becomes more exciting.

CHARACTER

I've yet to discuss how a director deals with character in the rehearsal process because I subscribe to the notion that character is largely defined by action, by what a person does and how they do it. A character in a play has no objective existence apart from the dialogue and stage directions. Focusing continually on character rather than on action leads to all sorts of problems, the most common being the oft-heard "my character wouldn't do that." Such a statement severely limits an actor's options. It can be especially harmful early in rehearsals, when an actor and director have only tentative ideas of a character's objectives, let alone who he might be.

When I directed *The Glass Menagerie* in Japan, the actor playing the Gentleman Caller fell into the trap of playing an idea of the character. For the first week of rehearsal, he had difficulty playing many of the actions I suggested—his choices were forced and colorless. He could sense my frustration. I finally asked the interpreter what she thought the problem might be. She conferred with him and then told me he thought the character's name meant that everything he did had to be gentlemanly! I laughed with relief and explained that the character's name is partly ironic. He's assertive and jocular, somewhat unmannered, and not always sensitive to Laura's feelings. The next day the actor was much freer in playing the appropriate actions. When an actor continues to embrace an idea of a character, it can mean he lacks the concrete behavior to flesh out a real person, or there's an absence of authentic talking and listening.

At the other end of the spectrum are actors and directors who believe that character is essentially an illusion created by casting and costume. There are, they claim, only words and—embedded in them—action. This radical point of view presumes that a director will always cast close to type. It breaks down when actors are not cast to type or when a role contains physical features that must be embodied to make sense of the script, such as Richard III's deformity. For an actor to pay scant attention to physical characteristics and behaviors is to accept the dubious Method strategy of playing every role as oneself. This strategy brings the play to the actor rather than the actor to the play. The way a character walks, talks, and performs even the simplest activities plays a critical part in defining who she is. Harold Clurman referred to this as the adjustment, the *how* of what a character does. Different adjustments result in varying portrayals of the same role.

For the director, understanding character and conveying it to an actor are two different processes. The casting breakdown presents a basic portrait of a character, but turning these insights directly into notes to an actor may occasion useless arguments about the idea of a character or generalized acting, or both. When the discussion focuses on action and adjustment, it is likely to be more specific and practical. Defining Amanda in terms of action, as a person who—desperate to hold her family together—wheedles and cajoles her son to help secure a husband for her daughter, will create a far more complex characterization than defining her as a generic "nagging, old-fashioned southern belle."

Another way of shaping character is to test the character in different given circumstances. Working with the circumstance that Tom has actually been frequenting the underworld would produce a very different character from assuming that his nightly adventures were entirely innocent. Making choices on the basis of action and given circumstances produces more concrete and textured characters than, for instance, labeling Tom as a sullen and introverted person or a happy-go-lucky guy.

The obvious question is when to focus on character. As you can see by the structure of these chapters, my experience is that starting with action allows the director and the actor to approach character organically. This isn't the only way. Laurence Olivier always started his preparation by devising a specific facial image for a character. This can work for an extraordinarily gifted actor who turns her insights into concrete actions. But for many more actors, settling on the externals of character before they've fully examined what the character does limits their choices.

FRAMING

When a scene in a production doesn't seem to advance the story, it's often because its key moments haven't been fully crafted. One of the director's chief tasks, in the middle of the rehearsal period, is to choose which moments to emphasize and how they are to be *framed*, or highlighted. Not unlike sculpting, framing is a matter of separating important moments from the previous action, sharpening their physical and verbal clarity, and giving them emphasis. While this labor-intensive process can start early in rehearsals, my inclination is to wait until the actors have had time to develop actions and absorb the given circumstances. Sometimes the problem with a key moment is not the moment itself but the absence of a solid lead-up to it. Although not all directors help actors find platforms for moments, doing so gracefully inevitably improves the work. In addition to key emotional moments, important information and plot points—such as the first (and sometimes subsequent) mention of an offstage character or event—also have to be highlighted. To stress that the information should be delivered with care and accessibility, directors will ask actors to "hand" it to the audience.

Framing is directly related to developing a production's style. It requires putting on the editorial hat to distill acting, movement, and staging. Questions that need to be asked include: Which character initiates or determines a moment? What is the moment meant to convey? What is its function? How can it further the production style? Utilizing the external point of view is the subject of the next chapter.

MINDING THE LANGUAGE

Although my thoughts about rehearsing language appear in this chapter, the words in a script must be closely examined early and continuously in the rehearsal process, alongside paying attention to action and given circumstances. As I mentioned in Chapter 4, if the actors do not fully embrace the language, the characters' actions will be severely weakened. Just as actors must particularize action and given circumstances, they need to make specific and personal every verbal image. When this process is overlooked or minimized, actors tend to barrel through or drive the text, as if the words were a barrier to rather than a means of communicating. In stylized plays, language is a primary clue to character. *How* characters speak—their syntax and its rhythmic properties—is an integral part of who they are and what they mean.

But particularizing doesn't mean deconstructing a play's language, or making heightened language sound colloquial. Like the parody of a Method actor mumbling his way through a Shakespearean speech, an actor may break up the language into bite-size units, relying as much on pauses and hesitations as on the words. Subject and verb clauses get pulled apart, imagery is difficult to follow and enjoy, and the poetry is lost. In effect, the actor has turned the play into her own vernacular, replacing the textual rhythms with her own. These tendencies are the result of either the actor's or director's lack of experience with heightened language, or the fallacy that one personalizes Shakespeare by treating it as everyday speech.

The imprecision of modern conversation makes it possible to understand a speaker without fully absorbing all the words, especially if one pays close attention to body language and behavior. But with heightened speech, all the emotional potentialities are contained within the words, not between or under them (in the subtext), and they can be released only if the speaker adheres closely to the linguistic structures. A character's actions cannot be clear and bold if the actor is inserting pauses and hesitations, keying the wrong words, and breaking up the natural architecture and rhythm of the text. Nothing is more important when rehearsing elevated language than making sure the acting occurs *on the words*.

When language is as complex as it is in Shakespeare, an actor's speech cannot be too clear. Besides continually stressing that need, directors enhance clarity through physical stillness and framing; too much movement can cloud the words. In realistic texts, an implied subtext often contradicts the words. With Shakespeare, the actor's personalization of the imagery and action must work in conjunction with the words if the language is to be understood. Acting truthfully is as important in Shakespeare as in any other writing, but it must be done within the linguistic design.

A close analysis of poetic dialogue produces a wealth of acting clues. You may already be familiar with one of them: onomatopoeia—when the sound of a word imitates the object or action being described. An obvious example is Juliet's line: "Gallop apace, you fiery-footed steeds, Towards Phoebus' lodging." To transmit the rhythm of galloping, it's necessary to stick to the meter as it is written, with the first syllable accented and the rest of the line alternating regularly between unstressed and stressed syllables.

Shakespeare takes the concept of onomatopoeia even further: the sounds and rhythms of the words underscore the emotions implied in a situation. In an exchange with Iago, Othello compares his "bloody thoughts" to the ever surging Pontic sea.

Othello: O! blood, blood, blood!
Iago: Patience, I say: your mind perhaps may change.
Othello: Never, Iago. Like to the Pontic sea,
      Whose icy current and compulsive course
      Ne'er feels retiring ebb, but keeps due on
      To the Propontic and the Hellespont,

> Even so my bloody thoughts with violent pace
> Shall ne'er look back, ne'er ebb to humble love,
> Till that a capable and wide revenge
> Swallow them up. Now, by yond marble heaven,
> In the due reverence of a sacred vow
> I here engage my words.

In *The Actor and the Text*, Cicely Berry illuminates the results of two different approaches to this passage:

> The long sentence from "Like to the Pontic sea" to "Swallow them up" consists of about six phrases which are all part of the whole thought, and it would be possible to speak them naturalistically making sense of each phrase, and break the speech up accordingly. In this way Othello would be explaining his feelings to Iago. However when we look further, we see that the structure and rhythm of the passage is totally related to the surge and current of the sea—there is more than grammatical sense here . . . If we honor each one of these small phrases, yet ride the whole sentence on one breath, we will come close to the elemental nature of that thought.

Even when a speech does not express a specific emotional state, its energy supports and enhances it. Once that pulse is realized, it provides the guide to communicating the richness of Shakespearean language. Shakespeare employs dozens of other poetic and rhetorical devices, many of which Berry analyzes in her outstanding book.

SPEECHES

Like dialogue, speeches are sequences of actions and responses. But because they often contain imagery and thoughts that are more complex, they have to be examined more intensively. Starting to coach an actor in a speech with a single objective in mind may not work if the details of the speech haven't been explored. There have to be clothes on the line for the movement of the clothesline to have any effect. Shakespearean speeches require the actor to learn the historical meanings and connotations of the words, often by using a special lexicon. A further stage is paraphrasing, which allows the actor to begin to make cumulative sense of the words. Paraphrasing, moreover, is part of one of the most important steps—specifying and articulating the character's thought process. These techniques, together with an attention to the given circumstances, will nearly always produce fuller and more complex actions.

Let's apply some of these tools to the following speech from Act Two, Scene Three of *King Lear*. The speaker is Edgar, Gloucester's "good son," who is forced into exile by the machinations of his treacherous brother.

> I heard myself proclaim'd;
> And by the happy hollow of a tree
> Escaped the hunt. No port is free; no place,
> That guard, and most unusual vigilance,
> Does not attend my taking. Whiles I may 'scape,
> I will preserve myself: and am bethought
> To take the basest and most poorest shape
> That ever penury, in contempt of man,
> Brought near to beast; my face I'll grime with filth;
> Blanket my loins; elf all my hair in knots;
> And with presented nakedness out-face
> The winds and persecutions of the sky.
> The country gives me proof and precedent
> Of Bedlam beggars, who, with roaring voices,
> Strike in their numb'd and mortified bare arms
> Pins, wooden pricks, nails, sprigs of rosemary;
> And with this horrible object, from low farms,
> Poor pelting villages, sheep-cotes, and mills,
> Sometime with lunatic bans, sometime with prayers,
> Enforce their charity. Poor Turlygod! poor Tom!
> That's something yet: Edgar I nothing am.

Is Edgar merely notifying the audience of his intention to disguise himself as a beggar? If so, very little of consequence happens to him in the speech. Monologues are nearly always about events in the past—such as Edgar's being hunted—but paradoxically, what an audience is really interested in is how a character will deal with the past; in other words, what is happening to him in the present. Having Edgar formulate the beggar disguise on the spot gives him a compelling thought process and provides the speech with a present-tense event of real consequence. A well-written speech is always about solving a problem right in front of an audience rather than being merely a narration of past events or an illustration of a condition. Notice how Edgar spontaneously conceives of the idea of the disguise and then justifies the strategy with his observations about the many beggars throughout the English countryside. Yet the latter part of the speech should not be delivered as just a pronouncement of something Edgar already knows. How much more interesting it is if Edgar is just now realizing how many poor people there are and how painful their plight is. If this realization is made part of his thought process, the second event of the speech is a deep developing empathy for those whose disguise he will appropriate.

Along with generating a specific thought process, an actor will need to be able to make the images of beggary specific in order to be able to see them before his eyes. And if the images are less than potent, he will need to find ways to personalize them. In the process of understanding the specifics of a speech, the actor will need to break it down into subbeats, where changes of thought occur, in order to tell the story clearly and build an overall action.

Like a scene, a lengthy speech has its own structure. Even if it has only one action, a speech can be broken down into subbeats. An effective rehearsal technique is to insert movement at every subbeat, to help an actor internalize the stages of the speech. Once a speech has been sufficiently explored, an actor must pull it together so that the main point can be made. In poetic plays, this normally involves coaching an actor to sustain a speech's long thoughts and long phrasing.

I find it best to work on lengthy speeches in separate rehearsal sessions. Rehearsing a speech when others are waiting around for the next scene imposes undue pressure on an actor. On the other hand, when a speech involves a listening character, it'll be difficult to rehearse without having both actors present. Often directors put all their energy into directing the speaker, only to find that the listener is bored or impatient. It is just as important to spend time determining exactly what the listener is listening for. Unless the listener has a strong need to hear, the audience will be equally as uninterested.

Working on speeches is enhanced by regarding them as conversations—either with an audience or oneself—and as occasions to work out a problem. Unless the actor has a problem to solve and a discovery to make, a speech will lack an underlying action. When the striving that produces a discovery is missing, the speech is likely to have little energy or purpose: instead of serving the character in the quest to accomplish an objective, it becomes merely the reporting of information to the audience, often in an artificial, declamatory style. An actor who has difficulty recognizing the discovery in a soliloquy can benefit by trying the speech several times very quietly, for herself, rather than being concerned with the audience.

Discovery is crucial to all heightened language, in dialogue as well as in speeches. It propels a play forward and injects a "lift" into the delivery of the language. Smart, clever characters who use complex language but do little discovering will appear glib and pretentious. And when there are no discoveries, the stakes are substantially lower. A discovery—such as Edgar's means of disguising himself—places a character in the thick of a moment, with something important to work through.

MODERN PLAYS

In plays that seem relatively realistic, some actors tend to discount the technical properties of the language. The director must guard against this tendency. Though modern plays are written in prose, most contain some heightened speech. Examining and embracing the language is essential to acting it. The style of Tennessee Williams, which is often labeled "poetic realism," nonetheless displays some of the strategies of elevated language. Here is an example from *Sweet Bird of Youth*. A faded movie star at the end of her emotional tether warns her young lover of the vagaries of age and fame. She recalls a nightmarish experience at the opening of her last movie—and attempted comeback:

> I made the mistake of wearing a very elaborate gown to the *première*, a gown with a train that had to be gathered up as I rose from my seat and began the interminable retreat from the city of flames, up, up, up the unbearably long theatre aisle, gasping for breath and still clutching up the regal white train of my gown, all the way up the forever . . . length of the aisle, and behind me some small unknown man grabbing at me, saying, stay, stay! At last the top of the aisle, I turned and struck him, then let the train fall, forgot it, and tried to run down the marble stairs, tripped of course, fell and rolled, rolled, like a sailor's drunk whore to the bottom.

Although this image is neither complex nor difficult to understand, speaking the passage requires respecting and embodying its poetic qualities, such as the sheer length of the first sentence, which conveys quite specifically the painfully long walk up the theater aisle to the stage. Breaking up the sentence by pausing after each phrase would undercut the agony of the character's journey. Just as precisely, the second sentence has the rhythm of a long cascade down the steps into humiliating obscurity. Notice how the long vowels of the first sentence—the *a* in "flames," and the *o* in "rose" —retard the event. In the second sentence, the hard consonants of "turned," "struck," "train," and "tried" emphasize the sudden violence of the accident and the actress's wild escape, while the *k*'s simulate the clanking of a falling object.

Deft actors will play poetry naturally; others may need to exaggerate poetic values until they fully grasp them. Regardless of a play's

style, actors can fully convey heightened speech only when they embrace the "object-ness"—the physicality and texture—of words and
thereby inhabit the language.

The middle period of rehearsals is also a good time to work on
giving texture to conversations by making the actors aware of how
their speeches build on one another. It's also a time to make sure actors aren't adding unnecessary pauses and handles to the beginning
of lines, such as "well" or "you see." These will disrupt the rhythm of
the lines and diminish their poetry. One of the director's many tasks
is to ensure that all the actors are riding the waves of a play's language
at all times.

TWELVE

THE EXTERNAL PERSPECTIVE
IN REHEARSALS

A t some point in rehearsals, an effective director makes the transition from acting coach to spectator and critic. By then most of the play should be animated and the key moments worked out, if not completely set. When run-throughs of scenes, acts, and the entire play begin, the director's critical faculties become his predominant tool. The emphasis now shifts to the external perspective (introduced in Chapter 4) as the director steps outside the framework of the house to inspect its joints and seams and view the entire structure. The external point of view opens up a template of structural factors against which the acting can be measured. The director hasn't abandoned the role of builder: she will continue to fill in gaps and fortify problem areas throughout the rest of the process.

Perhaps you've observed or worked with directors who, once the actors are off book, mouth many of the play's lines or howl at every joke. Anxious about their critical abilities and unsure whether the actors will fulfill the direction, they unconsciously try to help them along. It takes a certain amount of confidence for any artist to step back, assess, and evaluate. Young directors often ask how they can ac-

quire these skills, which they initially see as complicated and intellectual. For me, the answer lies in asking myself a very basic set of
questions as I watch the run-through:

> *Is this compelling, or am I bored?*
> *Is the story clear?*

I answer these questions viscerally rather than intellectually—and
then ask several more complex questions.

EVENT AND FUNCTION

> *Is there a significant event in this scene as it is currently
> acted?*

As you may recall from Chapter 4, an event is an incident or aggregation of incidents that constitute an entire unit, such as a scene,
act, or play. Since events are directly related to change and progression, what the above question is really asking is "Are there enough
changes in the scene to build a progression and therefore create a
complete event?" As long as actions and beats are plausible, varied,
and dynamic, there should be.

Using your homework, you can measure your initial idea of the
event of each scene against the work in rehearsals. The event of a
scene provides an excellent check on the playing of actions. With the
event of scene 2 in mind, you can make sure that the actions result in
arriving at the need to take action to secure Laura's future. Has
Amanda been able to persuade Laura that they must attend to her future? Has Laura convinced her mother that she has her own dreams?
A negative answer would indicate a need to revise or firm up the actions of one or both characters.

Notice how analyzing the event also brings into play the end of
the scene. Should Amanda have completely convinced Laura that
charm can overcome any difficulty? Probably not—it would be unre-

alistic to think she could. Both women almost certainly harbor some anxiety (their internal obstacles) about the future. But no matter how ambivalent she may be, Laura must accept Amanda's plan, or the acting will fail to fulfill the event—one of the chief functions of the scene.

You may remember that function is related to event but is broader in scope; the event may be just one function of the scene. When a play is schematic (formulaic in its storytelling), the only function of a scene may be its link in the narrative chain. In superior writing, every scene will also serve to develop character and relationship. The functions of scene 3 are to reveal (1) Tom's disgust with his job; (2) Amanda's terror concerning Tom's attitude; (3) Laura's fear of their conflict; and (4) the extent of the alienation between mother and son. In playing the scene, the actors and director must make choices that implement these functions.

CHARACTER AND RELATIONSHIPS

Are the characters multidimensional?
Are the relationships full and clear?

Character is another check on the choice of actions, which must be limited to the broad outlines of the role. Much of what defines Amanda is her intense, possessive love for her children. Without it, she would seem overbearing and unsympathetic. Selecting appropriate actions will make Amanda's love obvious, but choosing the appropriate action from among differing possibilities isn't always that easy. Sometimes the initial character ideas that the director prepared for the casting breakdown can—if modified in the light of rehearsals—serve as parameters for choosing actions.

Evaluating the completeness of a character requires stepping back from shaping the details of behavior to assess the actor's overall effectiveness. Ask yourself: Is there an arc to the performance of the character—a progression that culminates in a significant event?

Other questions should arise out of the same considerations used in casting the actor, outlined in Chapter 8. Is there vulnerability in the actor's performance? Is there humor? Most characters have some sense of humor, even if it's dark or self-deprecating. Humor is an important tool for creating dimension, vulnerability, and variety.

This is also the time to gauge the completeness of the relationships between the characters. Do the characters relate as if they know one another (if the play says they do)? Is there complexity to their relationships? If not, greater variety in their actions and more activities to amplify behavior are probably called for. Sometimes relationships are unclear or incomplete because the physical side has been left unexplored. One of the most telling aspects of a relationship is the way people touch. Physical contact is a powerful tool that the director must be sure to carefully and fully orchestrate.

ARCHITECTURE AND SUSPENSE

Is there rising action, or does the first part of the scene seem merely expository?

Are the turning point and climax apparent, or does the scene seem flat and undifferentiated?

Are the turning point and climax for the entire play strong and consequential?

Focusing on a scene's architecture is another way of ensuring that the actions are working and that the conflict is progressive and compelling. To assure an effective turning point in scene 2, Laura must disclose the existence of the boy who called her Blue Roses with a substantial, high-stakes action. For her part, Amanda must be genuinely touched and encouraged by the revelation, or the next beat—her "That's all right, honey"—will play as if she's giving up on Laura and is simply patronizing her, and her climactic speech about charm will be virtually meaningless.

To a great extent, *surprise* is what lends a story excitement. Along with contrast and variety, it's also one of a superior production's key ingredients. Surprise is often facilitated by suspense, which prepares the ground for an expectation to be met, changed, or reversed. A scene that lacks suspense may have too few changes in it. Or more likely, the actors are "playing the end of the scene"—and thus tipping it off—rather than performing actions based on the immediate circumstances. Even productions of abstract plays, such as imagistic theater, contain the surprise of when and how images will change.

Just as a director needs to specifically articulate the suspense of each scene, the acting must create and uphold it. We might say the suspense of scene 2 is *Will Amanda be able to believe in Laura?* or *Will Laura get out of Amanda's doghouse?* If the audience already knows the outcome early in the scene, either the actions are ineffective or there isn't enough progression in the beat structure to keep them wanting more. Even the most fragmented stories have a plot, which means they also have suspense. Being able to manipulate the plot—as one does when telling a friend a story—is a mark of a skillful director. Scene 3 contains two elements of suspense: *Will Amanda make Tom reveal what he has been doing at night?* and *Will she be able to make him stay and change his ways?*

Another reason that a scene may lack suspense is that the conflict is lopsided: one character's action is overshadowing another's. The suspense of the *Nora* scene is *Will Nora be able to persuade Torvald to give her more money?* As obvious as it is in the writing, the suspense can easily be negated in performance if Torvald isn't fully invested in teaching her a lesson about money, or if Nora thinks she can automatically get her way. Nora's overconfidence would result in her not working as hard to get the money, and achieving her goal would produce little surprise.

Even stories that start with the ending contain suspense; otherwise they'd be utterly uninteresting. Think of the many movies whose plots are composed primarily of flashbacks. Suspense works on many levels. Even when the ending is foretold, an audience may forget the information, refuse to believe it, or become absorbed in a hero's attempt to subvert it.

THE ENDS OF SCENES

A director usually attends to the ends of scenes just before and during the run-through period. Because the playwright has made each scene a unit, every scene requires some kind of closure, unless the action appears to continue or is deliberately anticlimactic. The ending may be a sharp ending—a "button"—a stillness, or even a trail-off. Regardless, it will always have to be worked in rehearsal. Most plays have a distinctive style of scene ending. The three-act American plays of the 1930s and 1940s often ended with a pithy line that was then punctuated by a fast curtain. In working on contemporary episodic plays, I will spend a good deal of time on the opening and closing moments of each scene. When endings and transitions are especially complicated, some directors will conduct an "ins and outs" rehearsal before the first run-through, focusing entirely on the first and last moments of each scene. This is sometimes called a transition rehearsal, but it isn't about refining the set changes. It is an excellent way for actors to (1) absorb the order of scenes, (2) figure out how they get themselves and their props from one place to another, (3) recall the given circumstances that trigger each scene, and (4) fulfill the end moments. Shaping the beginnings and ends is critical to establishing the rhythm and style of a production.

SHAPE AND RHYTHM

Beat structure and overall architecture are primary determinants of the shape and rhythm of a production, since rhythm is partly a function of the ebb and flow of action, reaction, and resolution. What complicates a production's rhythm is that each character has his own rhythm. Discovering and balancing these multiple rhythms is one of the more difficult directorial tasks. When a section of a play appears to have a certain rhythm or shape, try having the actors exaggerate it until it is absorbed into their natural playing. But always link your rehearsing of shape and rhythm to the actions, so that the actors have a "hook" for these external factors.

The style of the language can be a major factor in shape and rhythm. An extended section of single lines of dialogue rapidly alternating between two or more characters (called *stichomythia* in Greek drama and Shakespeare) has a rhythm that can be facilitated by eliminating any pause between the lines. This is sometimes referred to as a "run"—a series of brief lines that builds to a speech or a key moment. Determining and underlining its runs helps define a play's rhythm.

In the advanced stages of rehearsals, you can introduce the concept of pace without resorting to a general note of "Faster!" Scenes that have different rhythms (dynamics) will also have different tempi (speeds). Varying rhythm and tempo is as important as defining a credible speed for the entire show. Believe it or not, a fast-paced show

TIP: SPEED-THROUGHS

One of the best ways to achieve pace and cue pick-up is a *speed-through*. (A speed-through differs from a *speed line-through*, in which seated actors recite their lines for accuracy and for speed.) The actors, on their feet, perform the play as quickly as possible while maintaining the primary acting values and the beat structure. Props and vital accessories should be used, though full costumes are unnecessary. A speed-through can help the actors delete the fussiness of a performance by pulling together large sections of text. It also reminds actors of a play's larger rhythms. I tend to schedule a speed-through either just before technical rehearsals or just after them. Although actors may need to be reminded during the run to keep up the pace, the speed-through should take no longer than about 60 percent of the normal running time and can inspire discoveries even at this late stage.

may seem interminable if it has little variety in its rhythm and pacing. If the pace of a production is too slow, it's vital to determine what is impeding the actors. Is it a lack of speed, or is it the failure to pick up cues? These are very different problems. Often the pace will accelerate considerably if the actors "pull together" their own lines and pick up their cues.

ACTING AND STYLE

You may recall from Chapter 7 that shaping a production's acting style is a matter of distilling a vocabulary of expression. Throughout rehearsals, I continue to refine the production style by trying to describe it for myself in a phrase or two. Is it "heightened film noir," "a surreal nightmare," "a gritty black-and-white picture," "the poem of a young artist-narrator," "a Road-Runner cartoon," "a utopian fantasy," or "a hallucinatory cocktail party"? The more specific the description, the greater the chance of achieving a coherent style.

No matter how highly styled the play, I prefer to shape the vocabulary gradually. As I mentioned earlier, imposing your image of the style at the beginning of rehearsals may well curtail the actors' contributions and convey the idea that the authentic playing of actions is of secondary importance. My approach to evolving style is to explore actions while constantly searching for a vocabulary of movement and gesture that will intensify them.

RUN-THROUGHS AND OTHER REHEARSALS

Some directors utilize numerous run-throughs, while others schedule hardly any. Some prepare the actors fully for a run-through, while others prefer to startle the actors by suddenly springing it on them. At the beginning of rehearsals, I set a target date for a first run-through, sometime at the beginning of the final third of the process, preferably after a day off. This gives the actors a free day to finish getting "off book." Prior to the first run-through, time permitting, I like to run one act each day (and work on notes). One directing book states that the play should be run every day of the last week. This would not only wear the actors out but leave too little time for working individual moments. I try not to schedule more than three run-throughs in the last week, or two on successive days. I need a day or two between runs to rework those scenes and moments that cannot be fixed with verbal notes.

To get the most out of a run-through, the actors must be off book. They will inevitably call for some lines, but setting an early enough deadline for memorization makes a run-through more meaningful. A watchful director will figure out, before rehearsals begin or early in the process, which actors have difficulty learning lines. It's best to confront this problem early and head-on. I do this by scheduling line-running sessions for the actor with an assistant, just as I schedule rehearsals. At each run-through, the stage manager should assign an assistant to take line notes for all the actors. This is the only way to ensure that the actors become word perfect.

A run-through is not a performance. Props, substitute costume pieces, and temporary sound cues are usually included, but the director who demands performance-level acting will defeat a key purpose of the rehearsal—to give the actors the opportunity to build continuous life and find the overall arc of their actions. The actors inevitably feel pressure when the artistic director or producer and staff are present, so I request that only the creative team attend the very first run-through. Experienced directors know that rehearsals for a comedy go through a phase in which the play is no longer funny to anyone involved. While inviting others to attend run-throughs may provide some sense of how well the humor is working, a director with

TIP: WATCHING RUN-THROUGHS AND GIVING NOTES

There are two ways for a director to observe a run-through. She can see it as a protoperformance, worrying that every detail of direction is followed; or she can view it as a stage in the production's development—and as if she had never seen or read the play before. I believe directors get the most out of a run-through with the second approach. As I watch, I keep asking myself, "Is the story compelling? Is it clear? How can I improve it?" I apply all of the critical elements of this chapter while looking for the holes—the moments where energy drops out or the acting is generalized. The notes I take are of two varieties: (1) details in scenes I won't have time to work on before the next run-through, and (2) more substantial notes that will guide the rehearsing of the scenes that require the most work. Whenever we run the play, or even just a scene, I give some feedback to every actor. One of the most discouraging things an actor can hear from a director is "I don't have any notes, let's just run it again." Equally important is making sure to give some positive notes so the actors can trust what they are doing well.

taste and fortitude will continue to challenge actors to play truthfully and resist the temptation to "punch up" the comedy.

A pivotal decision is which notes to give verbally and which to give with the actors on their feet. To save time, some directors distribute their notes on paper. I do this only if a note concerns a line reading or refers to only one actor. Although they take time, group note sessions are important for two reasons: they are the only way to resolve an issue that involves more than one actor, and actors may raise important questions of their own.

Questions about which character controls a moment, as well as issues of staging, can rarely be resolved in note sessions with the entire cast. When a moment in question is critical or complicated, I save the note for a work session. Over the years, I've watched directors give the same note verbally over and over, not realizing that only by working the scene could a change be made. In making up daily schedules for the final week in the rehearsal room, I clear enough time to work moments in detail. By the final week any staged combat should be in the polishing phase and, if complicated, should be run every day.

VOCAL ISSUES

Clarity of speech and clarity of action go hand in hand, yet many directors only *start* to notice and correct voice and speech problems during run-throughs. This may work with some actors, but for most it will be too late. Although making actors aware of vocal problems early in rehearsals can put the cart before the horse, major issues of articulation and projection should be addressed, preferably by a vocal coach, at the beginning of the process.

A savvy director knows that projection issues are often really acting problems. Lack of projection is usually a sign that an actor doesn't understand or is shying away from a particular moment. Suggesting a larger acting choice early in the process is usually more effective than telling an actor to "be louder."

Once onstage it may be necessary to ask an actor to "fill the room" or "play to the back of the house" to increase projection. But not being understood isn't always a matter of volume. The problem can be excessive speed or a failure to articulate. A good way to avert at least some vocal problems is to make sure the cast has sufficient time to adjust to the theater. And as with acting notes, it's always more effective to point out specific problem areas than to generalize about an entire performance.

THIRTEEN

THE FINAL STAGES

TECHNICAL REHEARSALS

Here is a familiar scenario. You've had an excellent process in the rehearsal room. The cast is so enamored of you and one another, they're already planning your next project. The first day of technical rehearsals arrives—and suddenly everyone seems to turn into Mr. Hyde. Actors who had seemed level-headed now become jittery at the prospect of wearing complicated costumes, walking on a steeply raked stage, or dealing with the temporary cessation of run-throughs. Previously on schedule, the building of scenery and costumes has fallen behind. And reluctantly, you turn away from coaching actors to address an entirely different set of issues and answer questions from a multitude of sources. Yet in spite of these and other pressures, technical rehearsals can be exhilarating as long as you are prepared, steady, and patient.

Fortunately, you've laid the groundwork for a successful tech period by keeping abreast of the progress of construction, reading the daily rehearsal reports, and visiting the shops. The final props, some of which have already appeared in rehearsals, have been inspected and approved. You even attended a costume fitting when an actor had a problem or question, or a designer wavered between choices. I can remember going to more than a few fittings for a show in which the costumes were unusually daring. Had I not been there to support the designer and allay the actors' fears, they may not have had the courage to wear the clothes.

A prudent way of approaching tech is to make sure everyone has the same strategy and goals. Unless there is an inordinate amount of time, a *paper tech* is the first necessity. A couple of days before getting onstage, the director, designers, and stage manager meet to coordinate the integration of elements, map out transitions and the placement of cues, and set a schedule and rehearsal routine. Though unforeseen circumstances are bound to arise, a paper tech affords the creative team a head start by setting the agenda and allowing the stage manager to assimilate how the production's approach will be realized. The team also discusses how much tech time to allot to each act of the play, which problems may require stopping during the rehearsal, and when to schedule run-throughs and dress rehearsals.

I once endured a technical rehearsal of a student director who was insufficiently prepared. The transitions hadn't been talked through, and the stage manager didn't know when to interrupt to let the designers work because no strategy had been set. The director, panicking about the acting, would stop the rehearsal to give acting notes. Not only was organization lacking, the actors weren't given the time to become comfortable with the set and costumes. While a director should, for example, check the actors' audibility and clarity at a tech rehearsal, pressuring them to perform or concentrate on acting problems may jeopardize the completion of tech.

The way to get the most from this period is to adopt a relaxed, alert, confident, and positive demeanor—and acknowledge the contributions of the designers and crew. Finding someone to badger or blame creates unnecessary tension. Some directors limit individual designers to commenting on their particular production element— set, lights, costumes, or sound. But I think the best solutions often percolate from group conferences, so I don't hesitate to involve all the designers in discussing the look and sound of the entire show. (Starting this sort of dialogue back in design meetings promotes its success in tech.)

TIP: SPIKING THE STAGE FLOOR

Some days prior to tech, the key set pieces are placed on-stage in their precise positions so that the lighting instruments can be focused. The usual process has the stage manager measuring the distances in the rehearsal hall between the pieces and the edges of the stage to assure the same positioning onstage. While this method should work perfectly, in reality it never does because the actual set creates a different scale. Usually, a little tweaking solves the problem: a settee is turned toward the audience, or a table is moved away from other furniture. The stage manager normally makes these adjustments, but the director can make them definitively. This saves the lighting designer and crew a good deal of time. If the director doesn't see the pieces in position until first tech, an adjustment requiring refocusing will cause a loss of precious tech time. I always ask to be notified when the crew is ready to spike the set pieces, even if it's on my day off.

Tech rehearsals always start slowly. The crew and actors are learning their positions and tasks, and the first attempts at scene changes are usually tentative. In the early stages, it's advisable to stop and fix problems rather than move on. Once run-throughs begin, there may not be time to make major repairs. At the start of tech, I ask the actors to alert me or a crew member to whatever technical difficulties they find, and I assure them that all problems will be addressed. Although they may be concentrating on the production elements, the director, the designers, and the crew should make the

actors' job as easy as possible. Some directors make the mistake of trying to run tech rehearsals themselves instead of handing the reins to
the stage manager, who is in headset communication with the crew
and the lighting designer and is aware of backstage activity and problems.

Since tech is often the actors' first time onstage, some of the
blocking will have to be adjusted to the actual space. The scale of
and relationships between scenic elements inevitably feel and even
look different from the way they did in the rehearsal hall, where large
scenic pieces were represented by taped lines on the floor. An actor
may have to change an exit to be in a better position for his next entrance, or a short "cross" in the rehearsal hall might suddenly feel
twice as long. You might discover an area of the stage you never knew
existed or realize that the lighting can't separate the actors from the
scenery because they're staged too close to the walls (the same problem occurs when a background is painted in a color that is too close
to flesh tone); most important, the action that was visible to everyone
in rehearsal is now blocked from some of the audience. In a leisurely
tech period, there's time to devote an entire rehearsal to spacing, but
if the schedule is tight, the lighting designer can usually begin work
while the staging is being modified. In either case, major staging
problems have to be fixed before the lighting gets too far along.

Beginning directors usually take some time to realize that the
tech process isn't just a matter of working out an already conceived
concept. Tech affords a watchful director the opportunity to reinforce
the storytelling, refine the style, eliminate dead air, and sharpen the
rhythms. When I directed Shaw's *Mrs. Warren's Profession*, I discovered a provocative stage picture only when I saw in tech how wide
the set really was. In the last scene, Mrs. Warren, a brothel owner,
comes to her daughter Vivie's office to plead with her to be allowed
back into her life. Having run off to London to take an accounting
job when she discovered her mother's secret, Vivie is determined to
break away. Just before Mrs. Warren arrives to plead for a reconcilia-
tion, I had Vivie move from her desk center stage to a chair at the far
end of the room from the door. When her mother entered and sat in

the closest chair, they were at opposite ends of the stage with the entire width—more than thirty feet—between them. The picture told the story and heightened the silent tension. And it established a good starting point for their showdown by giving the actors somewhere to go—both literally and figuratively—as the scene progressed.

Tech normally begins without costumes. The actors shouldn't have to figure out how to wear and change clothes while they're still getting acclimated to the space and the lighting. The director and designers need time to adjust to each production element as well. In a three-day tech, costumes are normally worn on the second day. (Before that, actors can wear street clothes or parts of the costumes, avoiding white, which interferes with setting lighting levels.)

At the moment that costumes are introduced into tech, the designer and director must have enough time to evaluate them, or problems may never get solved. A parade of actors in costume used to be the traditional way of assessing wardrobe. In the professional theater, today's schedules often require that costume building continue during tech and even previews. More to the point, a parade doesn't reveal how the costumes will work in action. Though they are designed in conjunction with scenery, some pieces may require alteration if they impede the action. "Quick changes" of costume, while more manageable and commonplace with new materials, demand discrete time for the actor and dresser to develop coordination.

A sound designer rarely has time to wait until the middle of tech to begin working. An organized sound designer will save valuable time by doing most of his work before tech begins. Effects and music can be chosen or composed, cues temporarily placed, and a preliminary tape brought into rehearsal for the actors to adjust to. At tech all that will be left for the designer to do is set volume levels and modify cue placement.

Assuming you have faith in the lighting designer, you should wait until she sketches in a complete look for each scene before offering extensive comments. Most designers start by throwing light onto the stage, almost as if they were action painters. Constant interruptions make it difficult for them to try out their original intention.

You and the designer should have discussed before tech the look of each scene, its primary function, its focus, changes, and tone. Having an understanding of how qualities of light are produced greatly enhances a director's communication with a designer. "Can we try the 'up light' in this moment?" gives the lighting designer a much clearer idea of the desired effect than "I don't like the light on those actors."

Above all, the key directorial responsibility in lighting rehearsals is to make sure the actors' faces are lit. Taste accounts for considerable variation: not all directors and designers mind if speaking actors are shadowed or lit hazily. For several reasons, however, I prefer sharp light on the key actors' faces most of the time. It contrasts artfully with the surrounding darkness; the language becomes more accessible because their lips are seen; and it meets the audience's expectation (created by the prevalence of high-contrast film) that the lighting will pick faces out of the background. To the modern eye, sidelight, which sculpts the face, has become predominant. The flatness of front light makes it less than ideal as key light for faces.

Lighting should enhance the storytelling by reinforcing the play's changes and progressions. Synchronicity between lighting and acting occurs when the director and designer share an understanding of the play's important moments. One way to achieve this is to place lighting cues at beat changes. How scene endings and transitions are lit is nearly as important in establishing a visual style as how the scenes themselves appear. During tech an alert artistic team will continually uncover ways to support the production style.

TRANSITIONS

Accomplished transitions are critical to a production's success. Though they will change substantially during tech, they should be a part of pre-tech planning. Having a starting point saves time and energy and increases the chances of integrating the transitions with the rest of the production. A clever team may even be able to eliminate some changes by combining some of the scenery shifting

Before tech begins, the stage manager, in consultation with the director and the designers, often puts together a scheme for the crew to execute scene changes. Once they are attempted, the director adjusts and approves the look of all the changes. When shifts do not work smoothly after a few attempts in tech, separate time should be allotted to fix them. (Episodic plays will normally require additional scene shift rehearsals, even if most changes are made by actors.)

TIP: OVERLAPPING

The key to smooth and swift transitions is overlapping. The technique is not unlike a magician's: the audience's attention is diverted from the changing of scenery by entering actors, characters performing relevant activities, or multiple events. While some overlapping can be developed in the rehearsal hall, much of it will come out of technical rehearsals. (For examples of tight overlapping, listen to the way sound for a film scene often starts just before the end of the previous scene's final images.)

Limiting transitions to under a minute should be a goal. My practice also is to try to reduce or eliminate manual scenery changes. Even when they are cleverly choreographed, the routine of stagehands transporting scenery tires an audience. Regardless of the mode of scene change, it's worth remembering that grace is even more important than speed.

Transitions are about more than just scene changes. Like the scenes themselves, they communicate a production's style. Not all methods of changing scenery serve all styles. As you may recall from my approach to *Nora*, devising transitions should flow from and support the directorial approach to the play. Even when budgets dictate the method for moving scenery, the production approach and style must inform the transitions. Music can be a powerful component of a transition, communicating style and pointing the audience's attention toward the upcoming scene. When it becomes routine, however, music can make transitions seem longer. The keys to using music, as with any other element, are variety, contrast, and surprise.

AN OVERVIEW OF TECH

Each tech or dress rehearsal ends with a brief production meeting. The director and the designers give notes, review the progress, and revise the schedule if necessary. It's common practice to aim for a run-through somewhere between half and two-thirds of the way through the tech period, to allow time for repairs and one or more dress rehearsals. Sticking to the schedule for the first dress run-through should be a priority unless a "train wreck" ensues. Sometimes troublesome moments resolve themselves during a run-through. Besides, the actors and crew need to return to the play in its entirety.

Probably the greatest challenge in tech for the director is balancing the acting and production elements. Scores of shows that play wonderfully in a rehearsal hall are buried by design elements that don't support the acting. A director must constantly ask if the story is clear and the production elements are contributing to it. No matter how brilliant the design, it may be necessary to simplify or even cut extraneous elements.

DRESS REHEARSAL

At the final dress rehearsal, I invite a small select group to attend, recognizing that their reactions may not be representative of subsequent audiences. Friends will laugh too much and overpraise, while theater pros may sit on their hands. An actor once told me that open dress rehearsals in New York City often draw audiences of actors who spend the evening wondering why they weren't cast. Most of us have experienced an open dress rehearsal of a comedy that hardly drew a titter, yet one night later a paying audience howled with enjoyment. Nonetheless, an open dress can be beneficial. Adrenaline will drive the actors to fill and link moments, and the presence of an audience usually steers the director to a fresh understanding of the play and the performances. It's as if someone who is nearsighted suddenly locates the pair of glasses that has been missing for weeks. With the work finally held up to the scrutiny of fresh eyes, more pieces of the puzzle appear.

Although it can be unnerving early in a directing career, feedback in tech and previews from more than one source is indispensable. An artistic director who sits through tech and comments on every choice can make the process painful; still, as soon as there is a run-through, I'm eager for a response. At that point, practicality overshadows my ego: I'll accept a useful note no matter who offers it. Maintaining openness and equanimity, as I've learned from experience, is vital throughout the process but especially during tech and previews. A rocky run-through can produce a plague of uncertainty, which can be mitigated by remembering that very few shows fail to improve upon the first dress. When actors sense a director panicking, their belief in themselves will waver. And when the production is — or has the potential to be — good, a director's loss of nerve can cast a pall over the cast and crew.

PREVIEWS

Previews permit actors to adjust to the ways in which an audience completes the show and to test the finer points of their performances. Audience reaction to a comedy is critical in evaluating a production, which explains why successful comic films are so difficult to make. Running over laughs instead of waiting for them (when they are earned) discourages audiences from responding. Most professional resident theaters schedule four or five previews. In New York, because of a powerful press, two or three weeks is not unusual.

During previews a director must rigorously discourage "pushing" and playing to audiences. The natural instinct of some actors will be to embellish and extend dramatic moments, or broaden the comedy once laughs are discovered. Scores of shows play with great integrity early in previews, only to degenerate when actors indulge the audience's response. Although the difference between enabling an audience to enter the event and pandering to it may not be measurable, an accomplished artist has an unerring sense of where the line is drawn.

The preview period is a delicate time in the life of a production. Actors are sensitized to audience reaction and to a director's critical notes. With a production that is in relatively good shape, a director's job is to fine-tune moments, bolster confidence, and look for ways to extend and complete the actors' work. Equity union rules limit the number of hours for notes and rehearsal on the day of a preview, so a director must be judicious in scheduling note sessions and scene rehearsals. Some directors hold note sessions right after performances. I do so only when I'm trying to keep from calling the entire company for rehearsal the next day. That way, the actors who will not be at rehearsal still have time to mull over notes before the next performance. In most cases, I give notes the day after the performance to allow time to gather feedback and consider possible solutions before the note session. I'll still go backstage after a performance to offer encouragement, answer questions, and distribute a few notes to those actors who can't sleep without them. One has to be especially careful with general notes to the entire company at this stage. They can inadvertently place responsibility on the wrong actors. An egregious ex-

TIP: ACTOR'S HALF-HOUR

Actors use the half-hour prior to curtain to relax, focus, and prepare. Giving them extensive notes during this time is, I believe, inconsiderate. A thoughtful director will stay out of their way at half-hour or simply wish them luck. The exception is a simple logistical note, such as when a prop has to be taken off by a different actor.

ample is the common but largely pointless observation that the entire show lacked energy. Actors deserve more specific notes.

The stage manager needs to be present at note sessions, as they may affect calling cues. The stage manager is also responsible for maintaining the production and installing new actors, should replacements be necessary during the run of the show. When cuts are made, they should always be worked, if not onstage, then in the dressing room.

A dark secret of directing is the obligation at this stage to cut one's losses. This process is far more constructive than it sounds. Compromises are inevitable because no production is perfect. It's infinitely better to play to a production's strengths than leave the actors looking awkward. The director owes it to the audience to face honestly what doesn't work and do something about it.

You may still have time to crack a scene that has been inscrutable—with actors who are experienced and confident enough to risk giving up previous choices. It's even possible to rebalance a story by adjusting the emphasis and focus of certain scenes, although radically changing course now can be as difficult as turning around an ocean liner. American theater lore is filled with amazing tales of comedies and musicals that were completely rewritten, doctored, or redirected in a matter of days during out-of-town tryouts—and became Broadway triumphs. While this may work with shows that have somewhat interchangeable units (such as musical numbers or comic set pieces), it rarely succeeds with plays of any depth. Newly written or rewritten scenes can often enhance the production of a new play, but reconstructing a show would require another substantial rehearsal period. The impulse to redirect a play late in the process is usually a result of panic rather than considered observation. A production will never accomplish 100 percent of a director's goals, which is why many directors return to the same play repeatedly.

Paradoxically, as the director is evaluating and polishing the production during previews, he should also be weaning himself from it. Some directors find letting go to be particularly difficult, insisting on controlling every detail of a performance. This can only frustrate actors, who must now be empowered to take command. A balance must be struck between conserving a production's integrity and supporting the actors' efforts to amplify their performances. A basic precept of acting is that performances have to be slightly different each night. Expecting actors to be present at every moment also means allowing them the freedom to embrace the small changes in performance that are bound to occur each night. A director who objects to this type of variation will find few performances satisfactory.

OPENING AND BEYOND

No one feels more useless when a production opens than the director. An intense period of exploration has ended, and actors and crew now reap the rewards of carrying on a living event. The director leaves behind an experience of unusual intensity, in which a dedicated group came to rely on one another. Postpartum sensations are inevitable, but successfully transferring control to the company and crew may make these feelings slightly less acute.

Leaping into another project can be a beneficial antidote—and can also obscure the most recent experience. Freelance directors who make their living directing five or six productions a year rarely have time to evaluate their work or place it in the context of a career. I suspect it's unusual for a director to take stock of each production and its lessons. Yet rarely does an artist evolve without honest reflection and absorbing the response of audiences, colleagues, and informed friends. Knowing how the artistic staff of the theater regards your work can fill in the picture. Assuming that the purpose of art is to provoke and stimulate a considered life, it makes little sense for an artist to be anything less than honest about her work.

Although the press, in reviewing plays, may provide a service to readers, reviews rarely assist an artist's self-evaluation. Occasionally, a perceptive reviewer will offer a useful insight, but few can analyze a production's weaknesses. An agenda often precedes a review, which is why reviewers can be unreliable. On the other hand, a *critic*—someone who comprehends and appreciates theater, such as a Kenneth Tynan or Robert Brustein—can enliven and even elevate the art form.

Most artists know that reviews bear little relevance to their skills and aspirations, but few of us can resist using them to confirm our talent and obtain future work. (The case of newspapers reviewing student work is deplorable, since negative reviews are inappropriate and favorable ones can encourage novices to disregard informed feedback.) I recall a friend who, when he attended a show after it had been reviewed, would stand in front of the glowing notices posted by the theater in the lobby because he wanted to force patrons to make up their own minds. Such is our age's torrid romance with the media that—though it would be healthier artistically—one rarely comes across a theater that isn't dependent on reviews to entice customers. This situation makes it even more difficult—and essential—for an artist to cultivate a practice of self-appraisal. Equally valuable to one's creativity and serenity is the realization that a single production, whatever its outcome, is but one small measure of an artistic life.

PART IV

RESOURCES

FOURTEEN

THE DIRECTORIAL LANDSCAPE

As demanding and stressful as it can be, directing a play is a protected and secluded practice. A group of people decide to stay in a room for a month or so with a single goal, dedicating themselves to uncovering and communicating some truths about the human experience. Time passes quickly, and the world beyond seems a distant memory. This sanctuary is, for many, what is most enticing about the theater. But eventually the process must give way to a product that is affected by complicated aesthetic and social forces outside the rehearsal hall.

A book on directing would be remiss in not painting a picture, however subjective, of the context for the aspiring American director. Community and educational theaters offer considerable opportunities to direct—and sometimes excellent physical resources. Earning a living wage in the profession is more difficult. Those who do not run a theater or work as staff directors must take on multiple freelance projects each year, supplement their income by teaching, or support their art with a day job. Although not easy, these options are far more realistic than achieving the elusive Broadway hit.

If your desire is such that you have no choice but to direct, there are a number of ways to make a start. You can direct as often as possible in any venue, learn the other roles in the theater, apprentice to a master director, and intern with a reputable theater. But before setting out on any path, you have an obligation to search within yourself to determine whether you have the passion and endurance to sustain an artistic life in a sometimes apathetic and even hostile environment. Beyond having the necessary skills and personal resources, the directorial job description includes accepting the responsibility to uphold an ancient art and penetrate the world in which theater is made.

One starting point for the aspiring director is graduate school. With increased financial pressures on nonprofit theater, more professionals have turned to teaching. As a result, MFA directing programs have generally improved. Most schools prepare their graduates to teach, though a small number do train their students to enter the profession. While not necessarily preferable to life experience, these programs can fill in a student's gaps in a systematic way. Graduate training can, however, lead to overintellectualizing. For the past decade or more, theater departments have suffered from a severe disconnection between theory and practice. Where theater scholarship once addressed history, production criticism, and dramatic literature, many academics have turned away from theater practice to fashionable critical theories that advance certain social and aesthetic agendas, promote the critic rather than the author as the primary creative agent, and treat theater as an entirely intellectual exercise. To benefit from a graduate training program, a student must stay focused—amid the maelstrom of competing ideologies—on the practice and the practicalities of creating art.

Directing programs differ in emphasis and in teaching style. One program may focus on conceptualization and another on familiarizing students with the acting process. The intensity of the training can vary from hands-on teaching to independent study. What all programs should require of entering students is a thorough background in literature, history, psychology, and other arts. If stage directing is to avoid the predicament of film directing, in which the preparation of so many emerging directors consists of the films they've seen in the past decade, a broad-based education is a prerequisite. Without it, mastering one of the most important aspects of a play—its language—will be problematic. Nowadays, whether by schooling or by experience, a much greater variety of skills is expected than when a director's work was represented by the credit "Staged by . . ."

With or without formal training, a majority of professional directors emerge from somewhere in the nonprofit arena. Either they direct in a semiprofessional venue, or they move up the ranks of a professional resident theater. Until the 1960s, when the Ford Foundation seeded the growth of nonprofit regional companies, the proving ground was Broadway, touring shows, and stock companies. The founding of the National Endowment for the Arts in 1965 was a key catalyst for regional theater and the first sign in the country's history that theater was deemed worthy of national public support. Unfortunately, at the end of the twentieth century the pendulum swung in the opposite direction as the politicizing of funding contracted NEA support.

In spite of this climate, most large and midsize American cities have now established fully professional, nonprofit LORT (League of Regional Theatres) companies, as well as smaller theaters with professional aspirations. Though Broadway is the center of entertainment tourism, LORT has become the locus for the production of classics as well as new plays. Nonprofit theater supplies Broadway with its most interesting productions and provides a place for young theater artists to develop their skills.

In the midst of the remarkable growth of nonprofit theater, however, there have been distress signals. The financial climate for the arts at the start of the new millennium is precarious and has caused some theaters to rein in both ambition and risk. At many theaters season selection has been driven by recognizable titles or plays with a record of New York success instead of the passion of artists and the work of new and provocative playwrights. Some critics have pointed to this tendency as an indication that nonprofit theaters are abandoning their mandate and imitating commercial theater—and each other.

Fortunately, American theater as a whole has turned out to be more varied and vibrant than the criticism of regional theater suggests. Many theaters—large and small—have flourished while holding fast to their founding principles. Companies that grew up outside established structures have had a profound impact, from the Group Theatre of the 1930s to such contemporary troupes as the Performance Group and the Drama Department (both in New York) and Chicago's Steppenwolf Theatre. Meanwhile, first-rate regional theaters continue to produce much of the country's truly exciting theater.

In recent years, a serious concern about artist compensation has become a focus at the institutional level. The Theatre Communications Group, the umbrella service organization for regional theater, has joined with several foundations to institute a program of artist residencies designed to enable theaters to support a greater number of freelance writers, actors, designers, and directors. This seed program will have lasting value only if it sparks an even greater commitment to the individual artist from theaters and other funding sources.

Artists' economic health is directly connected to the well-being of theater as an art form, as artists must continually emphasize. In European countries, artists are often salaried and theater plays a more respected role in a country's cultural life. In the United States, the emergence of the regional theater movement has raised the prospect for the first time of American theater artists earning a living wage while working in the nonprofit sector. Yet the exodus of artists away from theater to the more lucrative arenas of television and film has been a harsh reminder that nonprofit theater has yet to fulfill its promise. It will be up to future artists to more consistently educate theaters and the public about the direct links between compensation, the growth of new generations of artists, and the impact of theater on our culture.

This is a tall order for future directors, yet if theater is to awaken to its true potential in American culture, the future artists will probably have to take on greater artistic and social responsibility. They will need to lobby more forcefully for the very principle of government support of the arts, and they will need to challenge the idea that public funds should be distributed equally to every state in the Union and to virtually any handicraft. Had the British government applied this principle to its funding of the arts, the universal appreciation of Shakespeare—a largely twentieth-century phenomenon—would never have occurred. American artists will probably always face a battle to demonstrate that art is not democratic and that taste, judgment, and value are essential components of artistry.

A healthy arts environment of the future will be one that promotes greater cooperation between artistic communities through the creation of a giant arts consortium that, like a political action committee, would raise a prodigious private endowment, proselytize the benefits of the arts, ensure student participation in the early school grades, and gather the kind of corporate support enjoyed by opera companies and museums. An arts superconference could launch strategies for educating the public to the crying need to humanize a civilization that is increasingly dependent on technology. Foundations would require that a minimum percentage of all grants be earmarked for artist compensation. Instead of competing with one another, dance, classical music, visual arts, and theater would work in concert to create a new climate for the arts—a broader and bolder reach into the heart of American society. And drama department theoreticians would renew their interest in the practice of theater by concentrating on dramaturgy in its fullest sense—not just research but the understanding of narrative as well.

Directors of the future will have to work harder to connect their art to increasingly diverse communities. By this I do not mean that their art should become more blatantly utilitarian; in fact, when theaters advertise the literal social utility of their art, educational outreach programs tend to garner more financial support than the art itself. What I am talking about is a much greater level of engagement between directions and actual and potential audiences. Many artistic directors have always embraced this level of commitment, but the impact of the art form is likely to expand only when the job descriptions for *all* theater artists include actively raising artistic consciousness. A lot of great theater was produced in this country in the past half-century. Too much of it failed to attract the attention and respect it deserved.

In an increasingly market-driven society, future directors must find creative ways to reaffirm the value of theater. A statement by Robert Lepage, the visionary Canadian director, made me realize how critical—and rare—it is for directors to proclaim why theater is in our nature.

> A man alone on stage, whatever he talks about, he talks about loneliness. Theatre is also about meeting, about not being alone. When Berlin was reconstructed after the war, one of the first things they did was to reconstruct the theatres, because people wanted to gather together. Theatre is a meeting point. Cinema is much more about one character intimately linked to another person in the room but theatre is the meeting of an architect and actors and writer and designer . . . That's why the theatre is this fantastic three-dimensional form of communication.

It has never been more urgent or more appropriate for artists to make the argument for theater. As each new technology increases our solitude, as the difference between man and machine narrows, the theater remains that rare communal place where experience can be interpreted and evaluated, where compromised ethics can be questioned, and where play becomes as valuable and nourishing as a commodity or an ambition.

Thinking like a director means believing in theater's ability to move human beings to see the world anew, if even for a moment.

THE NEXT PROJECT

A director's relationship to dramatic literature—a personal aesthetic—is a critical factor in determining artistic success. Since directors cannot really audition, they have only themselves, their productions, and their projects to offer. Without a personal aesthetic, a young director might be regarded as either overly ambitious or underread. Even if most directing jobs are for plays already chosen by a theater, the young director should draw up a list of ideal projects. This list is critical to developing one's aesthetic and translating it for others.

Thinking like an artist rather than a journeyman means locating and dreaming about a body of writing that moves you. It cannot be done over a weekend or on a summer reading binge. It is a continual process of recognizing and honing a sensibility and of relating dramatic writing to the world. Of all the art forms, theater is the most fashion conscious. Last year's hot playwright may today seem overexposed. *Mother Courage* was a superb choice to direct during the Vietnam War, but few artistic directors would be inclined to produce it in an era less interested in foreign affairs. Aside from the greatest of classics, plays go through cycles of interest and congruity, intersecting with the zeitgeist of some ages rather than others.

Although uncovering new work that demands to be done is a process unique to each director, there is no substitute for reading plays from every period, genre, and major dramatist—and attending as much accomplished theater as possible. It was productions by such directing giants as Ingmar Bergman, Peter Brook, and Giorgio Strehler that awakened me to what theater could accomplish and how an artist could connect to his material.

Some directors love language-based plays, and others favor plot-driven material. My own preference is for intelligent writing that has rich, complex characters. I would not choose to direct a melodrama set on a tobacco farm, but a play about a famous publisher and his children struggling over the ownership of a small family publishing company appealed to me very strongly. I tend to admire offbeat humor and real wit, as well as plays with strong stories and high stakes. Most important, if it affects me viscerally, I know it's a story I can activate. Whether a theater or playwright chooses you to direct or you choose the play, like an actor, you must have a personal path into a text.

WHY PLAYS ARE CHOSEN

In a university setting, plays are selected ideally as vehicles for training. At regional theaters, many of which have subscription audiences to consider, seasons vary widely in taste and ambition. They can be very adventurous, programming topical new plays or challenging classics, or they may seem more like summer stock, producing mostly superficial entertainment. Many resident theaters try to balance premieres with classics and modern plays, including recent successes from the New York theater.

Broadway musicals are not the only form of commercial theater. On a smaller scale, a commercial producer may want to back a playwright, or—more likely—a name actor in a straight play. Many commercial productions are actually transfers from not-for-profit theaters. Nonprofit Off Broadway theaters produce a wider range of material, though they too can be influenced by a package—some combination of a well-known playwright, actor, and director. Smaller theaters generally have less predictable reasons for choosing plays, which makes them more receptive to a director's proposals. If you have a burning desire to start a theater, it's all the more important for you to develop a personal aesthetic and an understanding of why certain plays appeal to you.

SIGNIFICANCE

Theaters often choose to produce plays that strike a contemporary chord. An obvious example is the work of Oscar Wilde, which, due to an increased interest in gender and sexuality, came into favor at the end of the last century. His play *An Ideal Husband* has regained popularity not only because its rights recently passed into the public domain but because its story involves the public and private lives of a politician.

Not long ago I chose to direct Anthony Clarvoe's adaptation of *The Brothers Karamazov*, which I felt spoke eloquently in many ways to today's audiences. Dostoyevsky has never really been out of vogue, and his novels have often been adapted for the stage. In the 1960s and 1970s, he was seen as a protoexistentialist. Enthusiastic readers of Beckett and Camus also admired *Notes from Underground* and *Crime and Punishment*. A few decades later, from a very different point of view, Dostoyevsky appears as a profoundly moral writer. The conflicts of materialism and spirituality, genetics and environment—what is passed from father to son—make *The Brothers Karamazov* seem exceptionally relevant.

Imaginative theaters are always searching for neglected or "lost" plays to expand the repertoire. Knowing this, a resourceful director will be an avid archaeologist, hunting for obscure work and continually rereading classics to see which appeal to us most urgently. With this in mind, I unearthed and directed *Spring Storm*, a previously unpublished and unproduced work by Tennessee Williams. I had little difficulty in interesting a producer in this "new" play, by one of the great American playwrights of the twentieth century, that spoke candidly to a contemporary audience through its focus on the anguish and cruelty of postadolescence.

Since the 1990s, the eighteenth-century French playwright Pierre Marivaux has had a remarkable renaissance in America, largely due to the work of director Stephen Wadsworth, who has now translated a number of his plays. "Marivaux's comedies," according to Wadsworth, "are really about the agony of change—the aspirations, the self-doubt, the yearning . . . Love, says Marivaux, gets you in touch with everything . . . Love is the key to self-knowledge." The way Wadsworth talks about Marivaux makes this previously obscure comic playwright vital and pertinent.

Given the intricacies of play selection, you need to be persuasive in advocating a project. Pitching a play to a producer or artistic director—with its connotation of two-minute meetings with Hollywood moguls—may seem mercenary and unworthy of being part of a director's skills. In fact, it's very helpful in developing an understanding of a play. The following questions are the starting point for a pitch as well as the in-depth process of thinking about directing a play outlined in Chapter 5.

TIP: THE PITCH

Pitching a play requires careful reading and considering such questions as:

- What does the play mean to you? What is the particular story you want to tell?
- What type of play is it? A comedy, drama, satire? What other play(s) can you compare it to?
- How would you approach the play? Would you stick to the period as written? Would you abstract or stylize it in some way? How would you cast the leads? Will your

production be a spectacle, or can it be done with a simple setting?
- Why should the theater you have approached produce this particular play? What is its significance? What does it mean *today*? How could it be promoted to an audience?
- Why are you the person to direct it?

Though a title or author can sometimes sell a play to a producer, the best way to persuade a producer of your suitability for a project is to do your homework. Announcing that "this play is great—it can't help but succeed" isn't likely to convince most producers. You will probably have more time than you would in a Hollywood office, but cogency is still a good policy. Producers are besieged with ideas for projects. They need to know, in short order, why yours is uniquely attractive.

SAMPLE REHEARSAL TIMELINE

The hypothetical rehearsal schedule reproduced below is merely a guide to the timeline described in Chapters 9 to 13. It is necessarily theoretical because variables such as available time, the theater company's requirements, the difficulty of the play, the progress of the rehearsals, and varying directorial strategies all factor into determining a schedule. This makes it impossible to propose a single all-purpose plan for all productions. A schedule for a production of a play like *Nora* at a fully professional theater might look something like this:

WEEK I

- Hold first read-through with full company.
- Second day: Read individual scenes, with discussion, and more reading.
- Uncover and test actions.
- Make concrete and specific key given circumstances.
- Build a structure of beats for most of the scenes.
- Sketch in staging.

WEEK 2

- Complete initial beat structures for remaining scenes.
- Complete preliminary blocking.
- Dig deeper for opposites and ambiguities.
- Work transitions.
- Work on key moments.

WEEK 3

- Refine staging.
- Start to frame key moments.
- Run each scene. (This may have started in Week 2.)
- Run each act (if time permits).
- First stumble-through of entire play.

WEEK 4 (In a tighter schedule, some of this work would need to be included in Week 3.)

- Work on major notes from stumble-through.
- Work on difficult scenes.
- Continue to refine framing of important moments.
- Run play at least two more times, with sound and as many final props and actual costume accessories as possible.
- Paper tech with designers and stage manager.

WEEK 5 (TECH) (Again, some theaters may start the tech process during the previous week.)

- Dry tech (without actors), if tech period is relatively short.
- Spacing rehearsal to adjust blocking onstage with actors (time permitting).
- First tech, focusing on set and lighting issues.
- Second day of tech; costumes usually added late in the day. Work quick changes of costume.

Third day or end of second day: first tech/dress run-through.

Half day of reworking problem areas.

Second dress rehearsal; possible invited audience.

Previews begin. Notes and work sessions in the afternoon.

Opening night.

POINTS OF REFERENCE

FROM <u>THE GLASS MENAGERIE</u> BY TENNESSEE WILLIAMS (DRAMATISTS PLAY SERVICE EDITION)

ACT I
Scene 2

Scene is the same. Lights dim up on living-room.
Laura discovered by menagerie, polishing glass. Crosses to phonograph, play record.[1] *She times this business so as to put needle on record as* MUSIC CUE #4 *ends. Enter Amanda down alley* R. *Rattles key in lock. Laura crosses guiltily to typewriter and types. (Small typewriter table with typewriter on it is still on stage in living-room* L.) *Amanda comes into room* R. *closing door. Crosses to armchair, putting hat, purse and gloves on it. Something has happened to Amanda. It is written in her face: a look that is grim and hopeless and a little absurd. She has on one of those cheap or imitation velvety-*

---

[1]While *Dardanella* was used in the professional production, any other popular record of the 20's may be substituted. It should be a worn record.

*looking cloth coats with imitation fur collar. Her hat is five or
six years old, one of those dreadful cloche hats that were worn
in the late twenties and she is clasping an enormous black
patent-leather pocketbook with nickel clasps and initials. This
is her full-dress outfit, the one she usually wears to the D.A.R.
She purses her lips, opens her eyes very wide, rolls them upward and shakes her head. Seeing her mother's expression,
Laura touches her lips with a nervous gesture.*

Laura: Hello, Mother, I was just . . .

Amanda: I know. You were just practicing your typing, I suppose.
(*Behind chair* R.)

Laura: Yes.

Amanda: Deception, deception, deception!

Laura: (*Shakily.*) How was the D.A.R. meeting, Mother?

Amanda: (*Crosses to Laura.*) D.A.R. meeting!

Laura: Didn't you go to the D.A.R. meeting, Mother?

Amanda: (*Faintly, almost inaudibly.*) No, I didn't go to any D.A.R.
meeting. (*Then more forcibly.*) I didn't have the strength—I
didn't have the courage. I just wanted to find a hole in the
ground and crawl in it and stay there the rest of my entire life.
(*Tears type charts, throws them on floor.*)

Laura: (*Faintly.*) Why did you do that, Mother?

Amanda: (*Sits on* R. *end of day-bed.*) Why? Why? How old are you,
Laura?

Laura: Mother, you know my age.

Amanda: I was under the impression that you were an adult, but ev-
idently I was very much mistaken. (*She stares at Laura.*)

Laura: Please don't stare at me, Mother! (*Amanda closes her eyes and
lowers her head. Pause.*)

Amanda: What are we going to do? What is going to become of us?
What is the future? (*Pause.*)

Laura: Has something happened, Mother? Mother, has something
happened?

Amanda: I'll be all right in a minute. I'm just bewildered—by life . . .

Laura: Mother, I wish that you would tell me what's happened!

Amanda: I went to the D.A.R. this afternoon, as you know; I was to be inducted as an officer. I stopped off at Rubicam's Business College to tell them about your cold and to ask how you were progressing down there.

Laura: Oh . . .

Amanda: Yes, oh—oh—oh. I went straight to your typing instructor and introduced myself as your mother. She didn't even know who you were. Wingfield, she said? We don't have any such scholar enrolled in this school. I assured her she did. I said my daughter Laura's been coming to classes since early January. "Well, I don't know," she said, "unless you mean that terribly shy little girl who dropped out of school after a few days' attendance?" No, I said, I don't mean that one. I mean my daughter, Laura, who's been coming here every single day for the past six weeks! "Excuse me," she said. And she took down the attendance book and there was your name, unmistakable, printed, and all the dates you'd been absent. I still told her she was wrong. I still said, "No, there must have been some mistake! There must have been some mix-up in the records!" "No," she said, "I remember her perfectly now. She was so shy and her hands trembled so that her fingers couldn't touch the right keys! When we gave a speed-test—she just broke down completely—was sick at the stomach and had to be carried to the washroom! After that she never came back. We telephoned the house every single day and never got any answer." (*Rises from day-bed, crosses* R. C.) That was while I was working all day long down at that department store, I suppose, demonstrating those ——(*With hands indicates brassiere.*) Oh! I felt so weak I couldn't stand up! (*Sits in armchair.*) I had to sit down while they got me a glass of water! (*Laura crosses up to phonograph.*) Fifty dollars' tuition. I don't care about the money so much, but all my hopes for any kind of future for you—gone up the spout, just gone up the spout like that. (*Laura winds phonograph up.*) Oh, don't *do* that, Laura!—Don't play that victrola!

Laura: Oh! (*Stops phonograph, crosses to typing table, sits.*)

Amanda: What have you been doing every day when you've gone out of the house pretending that you were going to business college?

Laura: I've just been going out walking.

Amanda: That's not true!

Laura: Yes, it is, Mother, I just went walking.

Amanda: Walking? Walking? In winter? Deliberately courting pneumonia in that light coat? Where did you walk to, Laura?

Laura: All sorts of places—mostly in the park.

Amanda: Even after you'd started catching that cold?

Laura: It was the lesser of two evils, Mother. I couldn't go back. I threw up on the floor!

Amanda: From half-past seven till after five every day you mean to tell me you walked around in the park, because you wanted to make me think that you were still going to Rubicam's Business College?

Laura: Oh, Mother, it wasn't as bad as it sounds. I went inside places to get warmed up.

Amanda: Inside where?

Laura: I went in the art museum and the bird-houses at the Zoo. I visited the penguins every day! Sometimes I did without lunch and went to the movies. Lately I've been spending most of my afternoons in the Jewel-box, that big glass house where they raise the tropical flowers.

Amanda: You did all that to deceive me, just for deception! Why? Why? Why? Why?

Laura: Mother, when you're disappointed, you get that awful suffering look on your face, like the picture of Jesus' mother in the Museum! (*Rises.*)

Amanda: Hush!

Laura: (*Crosses* R. *to menagerie.*) I couldn't face it. I couldn't. (MUSIC CUE #5.)

Amanda: (*Rising from day-bed.*) So what are we going to do now, honey, the rest of our lives? Just sit down in this house and watch the parades go by? Amuse ourselves with the glass menagerie?

Eternally play those worn-out records your father left us as a painful reminder of him? (*Slams phonograph lid.*) We can't have a business career. (END MUSIC CUE #5.) No, we can't do that—that just gives us indigestion. (*Around* R. *day-bed.*) What is there left for us now but dependency all our lives? I tell you, Laura, I know so well what happens to unmarried women who aren't prepared to occupy a position in life. (*Crosses* L., *sits on day-bed.*) I've seen such pitiful cases in the South—barely tolerated spinsters living on some brother's wife or a sister's husband—tucked away in some mouse-trap of a room—encouraged by one in-law to go on and visit the next in-law—little birdlike women—without any nest—eating the crust of humility all their lives! Is that the future that we've mapped out for ourselves? I swear I don't see any other alternative. And I don't think that's a very pleasant alternative. Of course—some girls *do* marry. My goodness, Laura, haven't you ever liked some boy?

Laura: Yes, Mother, I liked one once.

Amanda: You did?

Laura: I came across his picture a while ago.

Amanda: He gave you his picture, too? (*Rises from day-bed, crosses to chair* R.)

Laura: No, it's in the year-book.

Amanda: (*Sits in armchair.*) Oh—a high-school boy.

Laura: Yes. His name was Jim. (*Kneeling on floor, gets year-book from under menagerie.*) Here he is in "The Pirates of Penzance."

Amanda: (*Absently.*) The what?

Laura: The operetta the senior class put on. He had a wonderful voice. We sat across the aisle from each other Mondays, Wednesdays and Fridays in the auditorium. Here he is with a silver cup for debating! See his grin?

Amanda: So he had a grin, too! (*Looks at picture of father on wall behind phonograph.[2] Hands year-book back.*)

Laura: He used to call me—Blue Roses.

[2]In the original production this photo was a life-sized head. It lights up from time to time as indicated. The illumination may, if desired, be omitted. If used, it lights here.

Amanda: Blue Roses? What did he call you a silly name like that for?

Laura: (*Still kneeling.*) When I had that attack of pleurosis—he asked me what was the matter when I came back. I said pleurosis—he thought that I said "Blue Roses." So that's what he always called me after that. Whenever he saw me, he'd holler, "Hello, Blue Roses!" I didn't care for the girl that he went out with. Emily Meisenbach. Oh, Emily was the best-dressed girl at Soldan. But she never struck me as being sincere . . . I read in a newspaper once that they were engaged. (*Puts year-book back on a shelf of glass menagerie.*) That's a long time ago—they're probably married by now.

Amanda: That's all right, honey, that's all right. It doesn't matter. Little girls who aren't cut out for business careers sometimes end up married to very nice young men. And I'm just going to see that you do that, too!

Laura: But, Mother——

Amanda: What is it now?

Laura: I'm—crippled!

Amanda: Don't say that word! (*Rises, crosses to* C. *Turns to Laura.*) How many times have I told you never to say that word! You're not crippled, you've just got a slight defect. (*Laura rises.*) If you lived in the days when I was a girl and they had long graceful skirts sweeping the ground, it might have been considered an asset. When you've got a slight disadvantage like that, you've just got to cultivate something else to take its place. You have to cultivate charm—or vivacity—or *charm!* (*Spotlight on photograph. Then dim out.*) That's the only thing your father had plenty of— charm! (*Amanda sits on day-bed. Laura crosses to armchair and sits.*) (MUSIC CUE #6.) (*Blackout.*)

FROM <u>NORA</u> BY INGMAR BERGMAN

(A *sofa, an armchair, a decorated Christmas tree in the background. Scattered on the floor are packages and toys—a helmet and sword, two large dolls, a locomotive.*)

Scene 1

Nora: Come here, Torvald, and I'll show you all the things I've bought.

Helmer: Don't disturb me! (*Enters.*) Bought, did you say? All this?

Nora: But, Torvald, surely this year we can be a little extravagant. This is the first Christmas when we haven't had to skimp and save.

Helmer: We can't begin squandering money, you know.

Nora: Oh yes, Torvald, surely we can squander a little bit now. Can't we? Just a tiny little bit? You're going to get a big salary now and make lots and lots of money.

Helmer: Yes, but not until the New Year. And there'll be three whole months before the first paycheck comes in.

Nora: Never mind. We'll borrow in the meantime.

Helmer: Nora! Just suppose I went out and borrowed a thousand kroner, and you spent all of it during Christmas week, and then on New Year's Eve a roof tile fell and hit me on the head, and there I lay . . .

Nora: If a horrible thing like that ever did happen, I wouldn't care whether I had debts or not.

Helmer: And what about the people I had borrowed from?

Nora: Them? Who cares about them? They're just strangers.

Helmer: Nora, Nora, now be serious, Nora. You know how I feel about that sort of thing. No debts! Never borrow! There's always something oppressive, something ugly too, about a home that's built on credit and borrowed money. The two of us have held up bravely until now, and we'll go on doing it for the short while we still have to.

Nora: Yes, yes, whatever you say, Torvald.

Helmer: (*Takes out his wallet.*) Nora, what do you suppose I have here?

Nora: Money!

Helmer: There, you see. Good heavens, of course I realize it costs a lot to run a house at Christmastime.

Nora: (*Counting the bills.*) Ten—twenty—thirty—forty. Oh thank
you, Torvald, thank you. I'll make this go a long way.

Helmer: And now, tell me what my little spendthrift has thought of
for herself.

Nora: What, for me? I don't want anything.

Helmer: Of course you do. Come on, tell me. Name something
within reason that you'd like to have.

Nora: No, I really don't. But listen, Torvald . . .

Helmer: Yes?

Nora: If you want to give me something, you could—you could . . .

Helmer: Come on, let's have it.

Nora: You could give me money, Torvald. Only as much as you
think you can spare. Then I could buy something for it one of
these days.

Helmer: But, Nora . . .

Nora: Oh yes, Torvald, please do. Please. Then I'll wrap the money
in pretty gold paper and hang it on the Christmas tree. Wouldn't
that be fun? And then I'll have time to decide what I need most.
That makes good sense, doesn't it?

Helmer: Yes, certainly it does. Provided you really could hold on to
the money I give you and really did buy something for yourself
with it. But it just gets used for housekeeping and for all sorts of
useless things, and then I have to fork out all over again.

Nora: But, Torvald . . .

Helmer: No good denying it, my sweet little Nora. My little songbird is adorable, but it uses up unbelievable amounts of money.
Incredible how expensive it is for a man to keep a little songbird
like that.

Nora: How can you say a thing like that? I save everyplace I possibly
can.

Helmer: Truer words were never spoken. Everyplace you *can*. The
problem is, you can't. (*Laughs, wants to leave.*)

Nora: You haven't forgotten to invite Doctor Rank, have you?

Helmer: No need. It's taken for granted he'll be having dinner with

us. I've ordered a good wine. Nora, you have no idea how much
I'm looking forward to this evening.

Nora: So am I. And the children will be so happy, Torvald!

Helmer: Oh, what a marvelous feeling it is to have gotten a safe,
solid position. With a comfortable income. It's nice to think
about, isn't it?

Nora: Oh, it's wonderful!

(A final kiss.)

NOTES

Introduction

5 "an organizer . . . great lover": Harold Clurman, *On Directing* (New York: Macmillan, 1972).

I. Thinking Like an Artist

12 "The great . . . in life": Dale Moffitt, ed., *Between Two Silences: Talking with Peter Brook* (Dallas: Southern Methodist University Press, 1999).

12 "the person . . . the work": Arthur Bartow, *The Director's Voice: Twenty-One Interviews* (New York: Theatre Communications Group, 1988).

13 "Inevitably with . . . assert itself": Jonathan Miller, *Subsequent Performances* (New York: Viking Penguin, 1986).

15 "common sense . . . literary sensitivity": Ibid.

2. Reading and Researching

21 "You're a . . . better now": August Strindberg, *Plays*, trans. Elizabeth Sprigge (Chicago: Aldine, 1962).

21 *Second translation* . . . the scene: August Strindberg, *Creditors*,

vol. 1, trans. Evert Sprinchorn (Minneapolis: University of Minnesota Press, 1986).

22 "You are a . . . your worries?": August Strindberg, *Strindberg's One Act Plays*, trans. Arvid Paulson (New York: Washington Square, 1969).

22 "Is he . . . it better": August Strindberg, *The Plays of Strindberg*, vol. 1, trans. Michael Meyer (New York: Vintage, 1964).

22 "Sometimes it . . . rehearsal iceberg": David Johnston, ed., *Stages of Translation* (London: Nick Hern Books, 1996).

23 "It's a . . . of contribution": Ibid.

25 "I do . . . daily lives": Arthur Bartow, *The Director's Voice: Twenty-One Interviews* (New York: Theatre Communications Group, 1988).

4. External Analysis: Structure

49 "I asked . . . and son": Arthur Bartow, *The Director's Voice: Twenty-One Interviews* (New York: Theatre Communications Group, 1988).

63 "the contrasting . . . consecutive clauses": Cicely Berry, *The Actor and the Text* (1987; reprint, New York: Applause Books, 1997).

5. Developing the Approach

69 "The more . . . anti-verbal age": Michael Kustow, *theatre@risk* (London: Methuen, 2000).

71 "There is . . . understand everything": Arthur Bartow, *The Director's Voice: Twenty-One Interviews* (New York: Theatre Communications Group, 1988).

72 "The Wingfield . . . of automatism": Tennessee Williams, *The Glass Menagerie* (New York: Dramatists Play Service, 1945).

76 "By accepting . . . more striking": Jonathan Miller, *Subsequent Performances* (New York: Viking Penguin, 1986).

76 "I just . . . rhythmically *wild*": Stephen Wadsworth, trans., *Marivaux: Three Plays* (Lyme, N. H.: Smith & Kraus, 1999).

77 "re-envisage, re-imagine . . . *siècle* culture": Ibid.

7. Style

96 "Style is . . . the emotion": Stephen Wadsworth, trans., *Marivaux: Three Plays* (Lyme, N.H.: Smith & Kraus, 1999).

100 "the better . . . and sound": Jonathan Miller, *Subsequent Performances* (New York: Viking Penguin, 1986).

100 "The effect . . . Cranach's *Eve*": Ibid.

102 "I think . . . the inside": Charles Marowitz, *Directing the Action: Acting and Directing in the Contemporary Theatre* (New York: Applause, 1991).

102 "Style had . . . all-important 'externals' ": Wadsworth, *Marivaux*.

8. Casting

110 "decrepit old . . . pristine pride?": Harold Clurman, *On Directing* (New York: Macmillan, 1972).

9. The Early Rehearsals

136 "I would . . . becomes unconscious": Joan Herrington, "Directing with the Viewpoints," *Theatre Topics*, September 2000.

137 "adjust accordingly . . . stage picture": Michael Bigelow Dixon and Joel A. Smith, eds., *Ann Bogart: Viewpoints* (Lyme, N.H.: Smith & Kraus, 1995).

11. The Middle Rehearsals: Problem Solving

166 "O! blood . . . my words": William Shakespeare, *Othello*, 3.3. 452–462.

167 "The long . . . that thought": Cicely Berry, *The Actor and the Text* (1987; reprint, New York: Applause Books, 1997).

171 "I made . . . the bottom": Tennessee Williams, *Sweet Bird of Youth* in *Three by Tennessee Williams* (1959; reprint, New York: New American Library—Signet, 1976).

14. The Directorial Landscape

204 "A man . . . of communication": Michael Kustow, *theatre@risk* (London: Methuen, 2000).

Appendix I: The Next Project

208 "Marivaux's comedies . . . to self-knowledge": Stephen Wadsworth, trans., *Marivaux: Three Plays* (Lyme, N.H.: Smith & Kraus, 1999).

GLOSSARY

Action—the physical pursuit of an objective; sometimes, a tactic in an attempt to achieve an objective.

Action imperatives—the given circumstances and physical events of a play that need to be accommodated by the ground plan.

Activity—a specific physical task that may or may not carry an intention, such as lighting a cigarette or pouring a drink.

Adjustment—a particular change made by an actor (sometimes offered by the director) in the playing of a moment or scene; or as defined by Clurman, the way ("how") an action is played.

Antithesis—the contrasting of two ideas by using words of opposite meaning in consecutive clauses.

Beat—a unit of text wherein each character has a single action.

Blocking—the position and movement of actors onstage; also, the process of creating such movement.

Business—activity tied to props.

Central conflict—the opposition of the two central characters' major objectives in a scene or an entire play, often stated as x who wants a versus y who wants b. The rest of the characters and the themes tend to fall into one camp or the other.

Composition—the visual imagery created by the combination of the staging and design elements.

Convention—a consistent rule or practice; e.g. direct address to the audience.

Countering—the movement by an actor to rebalance the stage in response to a partner who has moved to his other side in front of and/or behind him.

Dramaturg—a specialist in theatrical history who assists the director in the preparation of a production and may also serve as a critical eye during the rehearsal process.

Dry tech—an onstage process in which the director and designers set light cues in preparation for full technical rehearsals with actors. **Paper tech** is an earlier procedure in which the designers and director (and sometimes the stage manager) talk through the creating and coordinating of the various looks and changes of the show.

Event—an incident or aggregation of incidents that constitutes an entire unit, such as a scene, act, or play.

Framing—crafting individual moments for the purpose of highlighting them. Not unlike sculpting, it involves separating some moments from others, sharpening their physical and verbal clarity, and giving them importance through emphasis.

Given circumstances—the background and present condition of a character, ranging from setting to previous action; the context for a character's action.

Indicating—acting that illustrates emotions instead of expressing action.

Meter—the structured rhythm of a poem, determined by the number and type of emphases in a single line. The meter of a standard or "regular" Shakespearean line is iambic pentameter, which contains five iambic units (or feet), each consisting of one unstressed and one stressed syllable.

Objective—a character's central desire.

Obstacle—the internal and external stumbling blocks to a character's pursuit of an action or objective.

Onomatopoeia—the forming of a word or words whose sound suggests its meaning.

Particularization—coined by Uta Hagen to describe the process by which an actor makes specific and personal all of the circumstances, references, and actions in a text.

Presentational—refers to elements of plays that call attention to a play's theatricality, such as direct address to the audience.

Representational—refers to plays or elements of plays that aim for an accurate depiction of the objective world.

Run—a series of brief lines building to a speech or key moment.

Sides—a portion of a play selected for an audition that features a particular character.

Speed-through—a rehearsal with actors on their feet playing as quickly as possible without losing the primary acting values and beat structure.

Staging—the final results of blocking; usually synonymous with blocking.

Stakes—the consequences for each character of achieving or failing to achieve their objectives.

Subtext—the underlying meaning of the dialogue; often a description of the characters' intentions and the action of the scene.

Variorum edition—a line-by-line compendium of various editions of a Shakespearean text; also includes notes and commentary.

RECOMMENDED READING

Bartow, Arthur. *The Director's Voice: Twenty-One Interviews.* New York: Theatre Communications Group, 1988.

Berry, Cicely. *The Actor and the Text.* 1987. Reprint, New York: Applause Books, 1997.

Bruder, Melissa, et al. *A Practical Handbook for the Actor.* New York: Vintage, 1986.

Clurman, Harold. *On Directing.* New York: Macmillan, 1972.

Dixon, Michael Bigelow, and Joel A. Smith. *Anne Bogart: Viewpoints.* Lyme, N.H.: Smith & Kraus, 1995.

Frye, Northrop. *Anatomy of Criticism.* Princeton, N.J.: Princeton University Press, 1957.

Hagen, Uta. *A Challenge for the Actor.* New York: Scribner's, 1991.

Johnston, David, ed. *Stages of Translation.* London: Nick Hern Books, 1996.

Kazan, Elia. "On What Makes a Director." Los Angeles: Directors Guild of America Newsletter, January 1990: 4–12.

Kustow, Michael. *theatre@risk.* London: Methuen, 2000.

Miller, Jonathan. *Subsequent Performances.* New York: Viking Penguin, 1986.

Moffitt, Dale, ed. *Between Two Silences: Talking with Peter Brook.*
    Dallas: Southern Methodist University Press, 1999.
Shurtleff, Michael. *Audition: Everything an Actor Needs to Know to
    Get the Part.* New York: Bantam, 1980.
Wadsworth, Stephen, trans. *Marivaux: Three Plays.* Lyme, N.H.:
    Smith & Kraus, 1999.

INDEX

action, 131, 153–54, 227; analysis of, 31–33; defined, 32–34; effect of environment on; and obstacles, 41–43; rationale for, 44–45; uncovering, 37–39, 130–32
activity, 33, 141, 227
Actor and the Text, The (Berry), 63, 167
Actor Prepares, An (Stanislavski), 44
actors: interactions between, 154–56; minority, 108; problems in rehearsal, 134, 183; *see also* casting
Actors' Equity Association, 120
adaptations, 24
Adler, Stella, 44
aesthetic, personal, 205
afterlife of play, 14, 77
All's Well That Ends Well (Shakespeare), 53
Almeida Theatre, 24
American Buffalo (Mamet), 49

American Century, The (CD-Rom), 27
analysis: of action, 31–33; of approach, 31; to language, 58–63, 98; to new plays, 56–57; to structure, 31, 46–66
Anatomy of Criticism (Frye), 52
antithesis, 62–64, 227
Antoon, A. J., 77
approach to script, 31–32, 69–72, 77–80
Archer, William, 20–21
archetypal patterns, 52–55
architecture of scene, 50–52
Arena Stage, 25
Artaud, Antonin, 98
As You Like It (Shakespeare), 53–54
auditions, 104–6, 112–15
auteur style of directing, 71
avant-garde, American, 13, 103

Barry, Philip, 27
beats, 35–36, 131, 227
Beckett, Samuel, 19, 50, 207
behavior, 32
Bergman, Ingmar, 13, 24, 41, 49, 56, 72, 79, 98, 159, 206, 218
Berliner Ensemble, 14
Berry, Cicely, 63, 167
blocking, 140–44, 227
Body Heat (film), 84
breakdown, casting, 106–8
Brecht, Bertolt, 14, 24, 26, 98
Brook, Peter, 6, 12, 13, 28, 72, 75, 206
Brothers Karamazov, The (Dostoyevsky), 99, 207
Brustein, Robert, 196
Building a Character (Stanislavski), 44

Cambridge University, 11
Camus, Albert, 207
Cape Fear (film), 84
casting, 104–16
casting director, 111–12
challenges, pinpointing, 63–66
Chaplin, Charlie, 103
character, 162–64, 175–76; and casting breakdown, 106–8; costume design and, 92–93
Chekhov, Anton, 14, 15, 20, 29, 33, 52, 110
Churchill, Caryl, 58, 85
circumstances, given, 35–37, 127, 129, 228
Ciulei, Liviu, 12
Clarvoe, Anthony, 207
Clurman, Harold, 4, 17, 110, 163
coaching, side, 151
comedy, effect of set design on, 85

compensation of artists, 202
composition, stage, 141, 144–48, 228
concept, 32, 69–71, 81
conflict, 46–47, 72, 80, 227
constructivism, 98
contact improvisation, 136
conventions of play, 79–80, 228
costume design, 32, 81, 92–94, 188
Coward, Noël, 74, 97
Cranach, Lucas, 100
Creating a Role (Stanislavski), 44
Creditors (Strindberg), 21–23
Crime and Punishment (Dostoyevsky), 207
criticism, 195–96
Crucible, The (Miller), 15
Cryptogram, The (Mamet), 57
cutting, 20

dance, postmodern, 136
Death of a Salesman (Miller), 108
Depression, the, 25, 76
design, 70–71, 80; collaboration on, 32, 71, 74; comedy affected by, 85; costume, 32, 81, 92–94, 188; first meeting on, 82–83; lighting, 81, 92–94, 188–89; research on, 81, 83–84; set, 32, 74–77, 81–85, 121; sound, 93–94, 188, 190–91; three-dimensional, 89–91; timeline for, 82
dialects, 122
dialogue, cutting, 121–22
Dinner with Friends (Margulies), 64
director: as animator, 6–7; as artist, 11–13, 15; as interpreter of play, 13–16, 31–33, 69, 77; as storyteller, 5–6

D.O.A. (film), 90
Doll's House, A (Ibsen), 24, 41–42,
    49, 54, 56, 79, 98, 159
Dostoyevsky, Fyodor, 207
Douglas, Lord Alfred, 109
drama: Greek, 13, 37, 79; Restoration,
    96
Drama Department, 202
Dramatists Play Service, 19, 213
dramaturg, 20, 26, 122, 228

emotional memory, 44
environment, effects of, 85
epic theater, 98
Eve (Cranach), 100
events of scene, 49–50, 174–75,
    228
expressionism, German, 98
external perspective, 173–83

Falk, Peter, 12
Fen (Churchill), 85
Fichandler, Zelda, 25
fight director, 64–65
Ford Foundation, 201
framing, 164–65, 228
Freud, Sigmund, 28, 44
Frye, Northrop, 52–54
furniture, rehearsal, 126

Galileo (Brecht), 24
Garnett, Constance, 20
genre, 52, 80
German expressionism, 98
given circumstances, 35–37, 127,
    129, 228
Glass Menagerie, The (Williams), 18–

19, 25–27, 36–41, 43, 47–51, 54,
    55, 65, 72–73, 75, 76, 79, 88, 98,
    105, 106, 109, 124, 127–31, 143,
    154, 157–58, 160, 162–63, 213–
    18
government support of theater, 202–3
Greek drama, 13, 37, 79
Gross Indecency: The Three Trials of
    Oscar Wilde (Kaufman), 92, 109
ground plan, 86–89
Group Theatre, 102, 202
Guardsman, The (Molnár), 29, 74
Guthrie Theater, 12

Hagen, Uta, 96, 124
Hall, Peter, 16
Hamlet (Shakespeare), 15
Hare, David, 24
Henry IV (Shakespeare), 78
Henry V (Shakespeare), 78
history: of other productions, 28–29;
    theater, 98
Holiday (Barry), 27

iambic pentameter, 60
Ibsen, Henrik, 20–21, 79, 119, 159
Ibsen's Heroines (Salomé), 28
Ideal Husband, An (Wilde), 207
images, reading play for, 73
improvisation: contact, 136; in re-
    hearsal, 156–57
In the Jungle of Cities (Brecht), 26
indicating, 44, 101, 228
interactions between actors, 154–56

Joint Stock Company, 29
Jungle, The (Sinclair), 26

Kaufman, Moises, 29, 92
Kazan, Elia, 4
Keaton, Buster, 103
King Lear (Shakespeare), 32, 168–69
Kopit, Arthur, 139
Kott, Jan, 28
Krapp's Last Tape (Beckett), 50
Kustow, Michael, 69–70

Lamos, Mark, 71
Landwehr, Hugh, 82, 83, 86, 89, 90
language, 57–58, 165–67; analyzing,
   58–63, 98; effect of environment
   on, 85; meter and, 60–61, 228; and
   movement, 144; playwright's idiosyncrasies of, 61; style of, 57–58,
   101, 170–72; and Viewpoints
   method, 137
Laramie Project, The (Tectonic Theatre Company), 29–30
Lawrence, D. H., 130
League of Regional Theatres (LORT)
   companies, 201
Lepage, Robert, 204
Lewis, Robert, 102
lighting, 81, 92–94, 188–89
light plot, 93
Lincoln Center Library for the Performing Arts, 29
Linklater, Kristen, 103
Lurhmann, Baz, 77

Macbeth (Shakespeare), 26
Machiavelli, Niccolò, 75
Major Barbara (Shaw), 62, 63, 106–8
Mamet, David, 41, 49, 57, 58, 61, 97,
   119
Mandrake, The (Machiavelli), 75

Margulies, Donald, 64
Marivaux, Pierre, 25, 76, 208
Martin, Steve, 79
Measure for Measure (Shakespeare),
   54, 55, 59, 61
memory, emotional, 44
Merchant of Venice, The (Shake-
   speare), 26
metaphor, visual, 75, 80
meter, 60–61, 228
Method, the, 44, 102, 165
Meyerhold, Vsevolod, 32
Midsummer Night's Dream, A (Shake-
   speare), 53, 54, 60, 75, 85
Miller, Jonathan, 13–15, 76–78, 96,
   100
Mrs. Warren's Profession (Shaw), 187
mistakes, directorial, 123
model, three-dimensional set, 89–90;
   white, 90
Molière, 37, 96, 119
Molnár, Ferenc, 29, 74
Moscow Art Theatre, 14
Mosher, Gregory, 49–50
Mother Courage (Brecht), 205
movement, language and, 144
Much Ado About Nothing (Shake-
   speare), 77–78
music, 94, 190–91

narrative, 55–56
National Endowment for the Arts, 201
naturalism, 99
New Directions, 19
New York Shakespeare Festival, 77
nonprofit theater, 201
Nora (Bergman), 24, 28, 41–43, 48,
   49, 51–52, 55, 76, 79, 91, 98, 99,
   159–60, 190, 218–21

Notes from Underground (Dostoyevsky), 207
notes, giving, 181–82
Nunn, Trevor, 72

O'Neill, Eugene, 86
objectives, 33, 40–43, 228
obstacles, 36, 40–43, 160–62, 228
Olivier, Laurence, 164
opposites, playing, 161
Othello (Shakespeare), 166–67
outward signage, 103
overdesigning, 84–85
Oxford University, 11

paper tech, 185, 228
Passover question, 157–58
patterns, archetypal, 52–55
Performance Group, 202
perspective, external, 173–83
Pinter, Harold, 16, 19
plays: afterlife of, 14, 77; analysis of,
   56–57; challenges of, 63–66; conventions of, 79–80, 228; by deceased playwrights, 14–15; framing moments of, 164–65, 228; interpreted by director, 13–16, 31–33, 69, 77; multiple versions of, 18–19; new, 15–16, 56–57, 137–39; obligation to, 15; reading, 17–19, 70, 73; in public domain, 20; in translation, 20–24; variorum text, 16, 229
playwrights, 137–39; deceased, 14–15; language idiosyncrasies of, 61
postmodernism, 5, 78
presentational, defined, 99, 229

previews, 192–95
productions, history of, 28–29
projects, choosing, 205–9
props, 126
Pulp Fiction (film), 84

quick changes, 188

Raisin in the Sun, A (Hansberry), 108
reading of play, 17–19, 70, 73, 121–22
realism, 75–76, 99, 142
rehearsals, 101; alternative processes, 135–37; day one, 120–23; day two, 123–26; decorum during, 132–34; dramaturg in, 122; dress, 191–92; early, 119–20, 126–29; external perspective in, 173–83; middle, 151–72; mistakes during, 123; movement in, 135; of new plays, 137–39; physical images in, 135; playwrights at, 121, 137–39; schedule for, 120, 152–53; speed-throughs, 179, 229; technical, 184–91; timeline for, 210–12
representational, defined, 99, 229
research, 25–26; effect on design of, 81; field, 29–30; on period of play, 27–28; playwright, 26, 28; on production history of play, 28–29
Restoration drama, 96
résumé, actor's, 113
reviews, 195–96
Road to Nirvana, The (Kopit), 139
Romeo and Juliet (Shakespeare), 26, 59–61
run-throughs, 180–83

Salomé, Lou, 28
scanning of lines, 61
scenery: changing, 91–92, 189–91; *see also* set design
scenes, architecture of, 178–80
schedule, rehearsal, 102
school, graduate, 200–1
Sears, Roebuck and Company, 27
Serban, André, 28–29
set design, 32, 74–77, 81–85, 121
Shakespeare, William, 14, 18, 20, 26, 37, 45, 53, 58–62, 76–79, 85, 96, 100, 101, 108, 110, 119, 123, 144, 158, 165–67, 179, 203
Shakespeare Our Contemporary (Kott), 28
Shakespeare's Romeo and Juliet (film), 77
Shaw, George Bernard, 20, 58, 61, 62, 86, 106, 144, 187
Shepard, Matthew, 29
Shepard, Sam, 58
side coaching, 151
signage, outward, 103
Sinclair, Upton, 26
sound design, 93–94, 188, 190–91
sources of inspiration, 72–73
space, theater, 85–86
speeches, rehearsing, 167–70
speed-throughs, 179, 229
spiking, 186
Spring Storm (Williams), 207
stage combat, 64–65
stage directions, 19
stage managers, 133, 187, 189–90
stages, 148–50
staging, 86, 140–50, 229
stakes, 158–59, 229
Stanislavski, Konstantin, 44, 102, 125, 156

Stein, Peter, 13
Steppenwolf Theatre, 202
story elements, function of, 47–48
Strasberg, Lee, 44
Streetcar Named Desire, A (Williams), 105
Strehler, Giorgio, 13, 206
Strindberg, August, 21
style: acting, 101–3, 180; historical, 98–99; production, 95–97; textual, 97–98; theatrical, 95–97
Subsequent Performances (Miller), 13–14, 96
subtext, 33, 229
superobjectives, 46
suspense, 176–77
Sweet Bird of Youth (Williams), 18, 82–86, 88–90, 171

table work, 123–26, 142
Taming of the Shrew, The (Shakespeare), 32
taping, rehearsal floor, 126, 186
Tectonic Theatre Company, 29
Theater Heute (magazine), 29, 70
theater history, 98
theatre@risk (Kustow), 69–70
theater space, 85–86
Theatre Communications Group, 202
Three Sisters (Chekhov), 15
time, 15, 75–79
Tractatus Coislinianus, 54
training programs, 200–1
transitions, 189–91
translations, 20–24
Triumph of Love, The (Marivaux), 25
Troilus and Cressida (Shakespeare), 100
truth, emotional, 96, 102, 154

turns on stage, 143
Twelfth Night (Shakespeare), 53
Tynan, Kenneth, 195–96

Vakhtangov, Evgeni, 156
variorum text, 18, 229
Vietnam War, 78, 205
View from the Bridge, A (Miller), 75
Viewpoints, 135–37
vocal problems, 183

Wadsworth, Stephen, 76–77, 96–97,
   102, 208
Waiting for Godot (Beckett), 79–80

Watergate question, 48, 159–60
Wilde, Oscar, 20, 58, 109, 144, 207
Williams, Robin, 79
Williams, Tennessee, 18, 38, 82, 97,
   171, 207–8, 213
Williamstown Theatre Festival, 82,
   85
Wooster Group, 15, 103
Wright, Garland, 12

York, Michael, 28

Zigler, Scott, 136
Zola, Émile, 99